Encounters

with
Heaven & the Spirit World

joseph martín

§Ŕβ

Also by
joseph martín

-The Origins of Elves & Fairies-

-Angels, Devas & Orbs-

Encounters

with

Heaven & the Spirit World

A True Story

Encounters
with
Heaven & the Spirit World

ISBN 978-0-9558573-2-4

First published in 2007 by Lulu

Revised edition published 2010 by Scarlett-Rose Books §Ŕβ (pbk.)

Typeset Book size Palatino Linotype size 12

martín, joseph. *Encounters with Heaven & the Spirit World*.
A Scarlett-Rose Book

1-3-0-6-2-0-0-5

www.josephmartín.co.uk

www.elvesandfairies.co.uk

§Ŕβ

A BOOK FOR

Joseph

Contents

The Background   1

The Little Boy   7

The Wall   26

The Park   54

The Room   64

The Real Moon Fairy   83

The Party   98

Conclusion I   111

Conclusion II   140

Final Thoughts   145

Chapter 1

The Background

This book arose as a result of unforeseen and phenomenal encounters. In many respects it was not planned or structured by myself, but rather formed naturally and spontaneously in response to the encounters as they occurred.

I still don't fully understand why I experienced these encounters. They are of a deeply spiritual nature, yet I would not have considered myself particularly spiritual at the time when they happened. I live a very ordinary existence, so these encounters could not have happened to a more average man.

All I will say, however, is that throughout my life I have been searching for answers to the 'big' questions relating to life and death - the same way I am sure many others have. Since I was as young as I can remember, I constantly questioned who I was and why I was put on this earth. I am fascinated with Nature and the Cosmos, and I believe strongly in the existence of God. I never truly thought, however, that one day my questions would be answered through the series of completely unexpected encounters I go on to describe in this book.

I chart the encounters as they occurred chronologically. The first of these took place in 1995. On this particular occasion I met with a small boy, whom I subsequently came to discover was my guardian angel. For many years, I regarded this special encounter as an isolated, albeit deeply moving experience. It took another eleven years, however, for me to discover that this was not a stand-alone encounter.

In 2006, quite unexpectedly, I experienced my next spiritual connection. This experience has shaped my life and outlook in a profound manner, and it marked the beginning of an intense six-month period of spiritual encounters which resulted in the writing of this book.

I hope the time gaps between some of the encounters do not distract from the most important themes or events in the book, as it is the encounters themselves and not their timing that is of most significance.

In many ways, I feel very unequipped and unqualified saying a lot of what I do in this book. I do not claim to be psychic, and am not able to tap into the Spirit World at will (at least consciously so). I never envisaged in 1995, or even after my second encounter with the Spirit World in 2006, that I would write a book about these experiences, nor did I anticipate being in a position to share such profound material with others. All I can say, however, is that I began to document these occurrences for my own records, but over time felt strongly compelled to share these wonderful things with others, in the hope that they might give hope or solace at difficult times like death.

I describe my spiritual encounters in as truthful and contextual a manner as possible, and was surprised about how well I was able to recall them all in such vivid detail.

None of the encounters occurred as a result of Near Death Experience or hypnosis, and I was fully conscious throughout all of them. The encounters lasted for varying lengths of time, and this is reflected in the length of the respective chapters in the book.

Although I have always been a believer in a Spirit World, I had never previously researched, read about or even discussed the concepts I go on to talk about at length in the proceeding chapters. Everything in this book stems genuinely from first-hand experience, and most of what I go on to say was completely unknown to me prior to the encounters taking place. My logical and sceptical mind constantly questioned and attempted to deconstruct many of the phenomena or concepts I met during the encounters. As I relive each event in the book, I share how I grappled with what I experienced on each occasion. There is a definite mixture of the mundane and the supernatural as I describe how each encounter occurred alongside my normal, everyday life.

A shift in theme and content occurs in the book as each chapter unfolds, and this shift happens as a direct consequence of the encounters themselves.

The first encounter with the *Little Boy* is followed by experiences dealing with Heaven and the afterlife, which are in turn followed by encounters involving the world of nature spirits. Indeed, unexpected and unprepared as I was for all these encounters, it was those involving nature spirits – verging as they did on the realm of fairy tale and mythology that most tested and challenged my logical beliefs and preconceptions.

I must stress at this stage that I can completely empathise with any scepticism, incredulity or doubt that may arise from reading through the details of the encounters. It would be easy for a sceptical mind to discount many, if not all of them, and this made me grapple with the idea of writing the book for some time.

All I can say, however, is that these encounters happened, and I hope that by sharing their messages with others, they help reveal something about the potential richness of life both here and beyond.

Chapter 2

The Little Boy

Before I describe the details of my first encounter, I need to stress that this event occurred (as far as I can tell) for no particular reason. I was not experiencing any emotional difficulties at the time, nor do I recall this period of my life as having been any more remarkable or noteworthy than any other, either before or after it.

As a result, I did not fully grasp the significance of my meeting with the Little Boy on this occasion. I had never really contemplated or considered the existence of *angels* before this, albeit that I did strongly believe in a God and a Spirit World. In fact, it was several months before I recognised that this Little Boy was very probably my guardian angel – something revealed to me through a remarkable twist of circumstances, as will become evident in the story.

The encounter occurred in early March 1995, and I find it effortless, even after so many years, to describe what happened on this occasion. My memory of it is still very vivid since it made such a profound impression on my psyche at the time.

When this first encounter took place I was living in an old house in the countryside. It had been the family home since I was born and I was by now a young adult.

My bedroom at the time was the biggest of three, and its large window faced onto the front of the house. The bottom of my bed was positioned nearest the window, with the top of it set against the back wall. To my left, was a large double wardrobe, and on my right, was a bedside cabinet and large mirror.

I was awoken at around 2.30a.m. on that cold, March morning. The first thing I noticed was that the temperature of the room had dropped considerably, and for some reason I found my attention drawn to my left-hand side towards the wardrobe. There, floating in mid-air, was an Orb of golden-white light. After having fixed my gaze on this object for a few moments, it began to change in appearance. I noticed how it began to expand from its centre outwards in both directions, so that it quickly became a long, thin, vertical beam of light - eventually reaching about one and a half metres in length from top to bottom.

The beam then began to expand again, not in length this time, but from its mid-point outwards, until it formed a diamond shape. The edges of the diamond were distinctive but slightly blurred, and out of this diamond shape now poured golden-white light, which lit up the area in front of it with a warm, golden glow.

I must have stared at this phenomenon for some moments not knowing what to make of it. I did not feel any emotion during this time, but was like a calm, impartial observer of events. I remember checking to ensure I was completely conscious and recall noting that my eyes were wide awake. I was able to feel the cold air in the room to such an extent that I could now see the coldness on my breath when I exhaled.

It was suddenly at this moment that the vision became much more profound in content.

I beheld a figure set within the light of the diamond. It began to emerge outwards from within the light until it eventually moved out of the diamond structure. The figure did not walk or move as an ordinary human would, but rather glided out slightly above the ground, surrounded all the time by a golden-white mist. It moved out of the diamond structure a sufficient distance, and I was now able to see it in much greater detail.

There in front of me was a young boy aged approximately six to eight years old. He had wavy, blonde hair that was just short of his shoulders in length. His hair framed his forehead, and curled and weaved around his ears. His eyes were an intense blue colour and contrasted sharply with his very soft, pearly-white complexion.

The Little Boy had a smile that exuded a feeling of warmth, gentleness and peacefulness I had never before (or since) experienced. It was an enigmatic smile; his lips remained closed at all times, so he never revealed any teeth. I found myself immediately comforted by the beautiful, peaceful and calm aura which entered the room along with him.

I now began to look more closely at the Little Boy's appearance and attire. He wore a white satin shirt, whose laced collar folded softly over the edges of his turquoise jacket. The jacket had a unique design and wasn't modern in style. It was made from turquoise satin, and had turquoise satin buttons which were fastened by small loops made from the same fabric. The jacket was waist-length, very neatly fitted, and its arms were short enough to reveal the laced cuffs of his shirt underneath.

The *'Little Boy'* (as I fondly came to know him) also wore pantaloons made from the same turquoise satin material. I could not see his footwear, however, due to the glow from the golden-white light which surrounded his body. His clothes very much reminded me of those from around the time of the English Civil War.

The Little Boy remained for some time at the bottom of my bed smiling at me. Then quietly, in a matter of fact way, I decided to ask him what he wanted. There was neither reply in word nor gesture, and the Little Boy simply remained quiet, all the time radiating gentleness and love.

I checked again to see if I was conscious, and observed the coldness on my breath. Sceptically, I decided to pinch myself to make sure I was fully awake. I resolved to do this regularly, so that I would not be 'tricked' into seeing something that might not actually be there at all.

As I was going through this strategy in my head, I now observed the Little Boy gliding slowly and deliberately back into the diamond structure. I was able to watch as the diamond shape folded gradually back into the long, golden-white beam of light, which in turn collapsed slowly and simultaneously from both top and bottom, and once again became the Orb of golden light that had first appeared in the room. The Orb then simply disappeared from whence it came. I stared into the now empty space in front of me for a time and then closed my eyes and calmly fell asleep.

At approximately 4.00a.m. I awoke and found total silence inside the bedroom. I looked towards my left-hand side where the wardrobe was and suddenly recalled the events of earlier that morning. To my amazement, there once more appeared the small Orb of pulsating, golden-white light.

I couldn't hear any noise from inside the Orb, but simply watched it as it began to expand once more into the by now familiar long, thin beam of light, and then into the diamond structure.

Again, the quantity and intensity of light emanating from the diamond shape illuminated most of the room in front of it.

This time, however, I noticed something slightly different about the golden-white light. It now appeared to encase part of the room within some sort of protective bubble, where *time* did not, nor could not exist. It didn't seem as though time had stopped or slowed down inside the bubble, but I really felt that it didn't operate there at all. I was now in a different time dimension, outside ordinary reality. This phenomenon only occurred inside the light bubble, which encapsulated my bed, the back wall and parts of the two sidewalls. The wall where the bedroom window was did not seem to be affected, and I sensed that ordinary time did exist there, outside the casing of the light bubble.

This sensation of timelessness served to further heighten and intensify the atmosphere of peacefulness and happiness which had characterised my first encounter with the Little Boy only hours previously.

I looked into the diamond structure once more, but the golden-white light was so brilliant that I initially saw nothing. A moment or two later, however, out glided the Little Boy, but this time he appeared to materialise out of the actual light, as though he was some sort of light manifestation himself. As I looked on, the Little Boy moved up to the bottom, left-hand side of my bed and remained there with his wonderful, gentle smile. It was unmistakably the same Little Boy who had appeared to me earlier that night. I found myself staring at him in awe, but this time I was more prepared to interact with him.

It occurred to me to gauge my level of consciousness by pinching myself, as I had resolved to do earlier that night. I did this twice, and again observed the coolness on my breath. I decided to try communicating with the Little Boy, so I quietly asked him who he was and what he wanted. Just as before, the Little Boy simply looked at me and smiled quietly with his gentle, comforting radiance.

With no answers forthcoming, I tried to pinch my left arm to check again that I was still awake. I did this several times, but noticed how I couldn't feel any physical sensation. I didn't look at what I was doing because I couldn't take my gaze off the Little Boy. One more time, I softly said to him, *"Hello"* and *"What do you want?"*, but still I got no answer.

Then, suddenly and intuitively, I realised this meeting was about to finally end. No-one spoke to me, but I sensed almost telepathically that this was the case. Sure enough, the Little Boy then began to glide back into the diamond structure; he took the bubble of light with him, and appeared to become 'One' with its light energy once more.

The diamond shape then collapsed into the beam of light, which further collapsed into the Orb of golden-white light. After a few moments, the

Orb slowly dematerialised and the bedroom fell back into silent darkness. I thought nothing more about this event for now, and slipped into a peaceful sleep once again.

I awoke early the next morning and got up for work as normal. Before having breakfast, I went to have my usual shower, but just prior to this, I looked down at my arm at the area near my wrist. I noticed immediately how it was rather bruised and appeared to have been scratched quite badly. I realised straight away that I must have caused this on the previous night, and slowly found myself recalling my encounter with the Little Boy.

As I did this, I smiled ironically at the entire situation, thinking I had probably been very silly imagining that a '*Little Boy*' had come to visit me. I pushed these thoughts to the back of my head, had my shower, ate my breakfast and went to work, not realising that this story was far from over.

Days, weeks and months passed. I had almost totally forgotten about the 'dream' of the

Little Boy - his warm, tranquil smile, and the lovely aura which had accompanied him.

During these months I was extremely busy since I had decided to sell my house and move into a new one some miles away. Everything went well with the move and I set about organising my new home by late July 1995.

The summer of 1995 was very warm and sunny, and I enjoyed the several weeks I had to decorate. I was playing a lot of golf at the time and decided to get satellite television installed, specifically because I wanted to watch the Ryder Cup from Oak Hill Country Club, Rochester, N.Y. later on that summer.

Friday 25th August came and I recall it was another beautiful, warm and sunny day. It was early afternoon, so I decided to have a cup of tea and watch some television.

I was casually browsing some of the channels I was still largely unfamiliar with, and happened upon one where a documentary had already started. I didn't take care to note the name or nature of this documentary, but simply settled down and began to watch it for some strange reason.

A story was being re-enacted, and I recall the events it portrayed vividly. It concerned the story of a woman (from America) whose life had been successful and happy up until the sudden illness and death of her husband. The woman was so engulfed with grief, she let her estate fall into ruin. She became a 'bag lady', and found herself walking the streets of some town or city. She lived off what she could find, and pushed around an old trolley which contained all her remaining belongings. The woman slept rough at night since she had nowhere to go, nor did she have any friends to talk to. All that had ever mattered to her in life, her deceased husband, had now gone.

Part of the woman's routine included visiting local charity stores to look for clothes. One of those in question was an old '*War-on-Want*' store, and she often frequented it because she had become quite friendly with its female owner, who regularly donated her clothes.

The documentary proceeded to re-enact the events of one particular day when the lady had visited the store. She greeted the owner, who informed her that she had some clothes for her to try on, and directed her to one of the fitting rooms at the back of the premises. The old lady duly went over to the fitting rooms, and after about ten minutes or so, walked back to the counter where the owner was still standing. The owner had told the old lady that if any of the clothes were suitable, she could keep them at no cost.

The old lady as always felt very grateful for such kindness from someone who was essentially unconnected to her by way of family or formal friendship.

But it was what transpired next in this story that really captured my attention. I attempt to recall the dialogue between the two women as best

I can in order to recount how this fascinating tale unfolded.

The old lady thanked the owner for the clothes once more, but this time she also turned to her and said, "Tell your nephew thank you so much for his help. He was really very wonderful and kind in helping me choose the clothes that best suited."

The store owner reacted with bewilderment at what the old lady was saying. She replied, "I really don't know what you're talking about, because I don't have a nephew." The old lady insisted however, "There was a little boy who helped me choose clothes in your fitting room. I assumed he was a relation of yours, because he was so kind and helpful."

The owner then began to get slightly worried. She went to the back of the store where the fitting rooms were situated, but found no trace of *anyone*, never mind a small boy. The owner stressed to the old lady that she must have imagined this child. She informed her that there was only one way into the store, and she was definite no one had passed her as she had stood by the till at the door.

The old lady was adamant, however, that a young boy was in the fitting room and had helped her decide what clothes to wear.

At this point, the owner became overly alarmed and decided the best course of action was to call the police. After a while, the police came and took statements from both women. They also brought with them a sketch artist in order to obtain an image of the 'suspect' child.

It was what unfolded next, however, that changed my entire outlook, not just in relation to the story being recounted in the documentary, but also in respect of my encounter with the Little Boy some months previously.

After the police sketch artist had finished his drawing of the suspect boy, he showed the picture to the old woman, who confirmed that the sketch definitely resembled the boy who had helped her choose clothes earlier that day.

The television camera then panned in on the sketch, and what I beheld was nearly enough to make me fall off my seat in shocked disbelief.

There, on the television screen, was the image of the young boy who had appeared to the old lady. Unbelievably, however, it was also the image of the Little Boy who had appeared in my bedroom some months ago.

I just couldn't believe it. This was indeed the same Little Boy, with the intense blue eyes and wavy blonde hair, wearing the same turquoise silk outfit of old. The sketch artist's picture brought back all the memories of the Little Boy I had encountered five months previously.

As I proceeded to watch on with heightened curiosity, I discovered the documentary's theme or focus was '*angels*', particularly '*guardian angels*'.

It transpired that the Little Boy had appeared to several people across America. They each believed he had visited them in order to help or assist them in some way. Three or four people were interviewed in respect of having encountered this Little Boy, and they were all convinced he was their *guardian angel.*

The documentary revealed that the Little Boy had affected the two women in the charity store so profoundly, the owner later gave the old lady a permanent job as manageress. When the owner eventually retired, the old lady became the new owner, and subsequently went on to help other people living off the streets. This Little Boy obviously had a profound and life-changing effect on both women.

I simply couldn't believe what I had just seen and heard. I now found myself remembering the Little Boy's face and clothes, and finally admitted to myself that my encounter with him earlier that year had not been a dream. I now knew it had marked one of the most privileged, spiritual experiences of my entire life. I began to recognise that I had probably met my own guardian angel or guide, and realised he had been trying to tell me that he was always there to help.

I suddenly felt an overwhelming emotion of gratitude and love for this caring and awe-inspiring entity. But why, I asked, had he come to me? I was very happy and not worried about anything in life. What did all of this mean? Was it a good sign or a bad sign? All I could recall was that the Little Boy had brought with him an intense feeling of calm, peacefulness and happiness.

In the intervening years, I recounted the story of the Little Boy to some close friends, and explained to them why I believed he was my guardian angel. Little did I realise, however, it would take another eleven years for me to discover *why* the Little Boy had come to visit me that night in March 1995.

I go on to reveal the true and lasting significance of this encounter in the next few chapters of the book.

Chapter 3

The Wall

The cherished memory of my encounter with the *Little Boy* remained with me for many years, but I always presumed this would be an isolated experience.

Almost eleven years exactly to the day, however, my attention was drawn once more to the Spirit World in a most dramatic and unexpected manner.

By this time my life had changed quite significantly. I was by now happily married and had moved house once again. These positive events, however, had been directly preceded by an intensely challenging period of two to three years, but it now seemed that the darker clouds had finally lifted, and my life once more assumed a positive outlook.

What I go on to speak about in this chapter is based upon the vivid memories I retained of this encounter, and its details are taken from notes I made in relation to the 'messages' I received during it.

I must stress that all the information I include here was obtained wholly through some form of imparted knowledge; I presume this came from a Heavenly or Spiritual source. It was not actually spoken to me, but all I can say is I did not possess any of this understanding until I experienced the actual encounter in question. I had never previously read about, researched or even contemplated any of the themes or information I acquired through it. Many of the things I found myself believing about the Spirit World or Heaven after this encounter were the complete opposite of what I had presumed or believed about them prior to it taking place.

Since having this encounter, I have read and researched a variety of material relating to the spiritual themes which arose from it. In some cases, I have found uncanny similarities between what other writers and I say about the Spirit World, whilst in others I have found total disparity. It is not the place of this book to mention the work or ideas of others, nor is it appropriate for me to draw comparisons between their experiences and mine. What I go on to describe here is taken genuinely and directly from *first-hand* experience.

The encounter in this chapter occurred directly after the death of one of my old acquaintances, Harry.

Harry died one morning in the spring of 2006 after having fought an illness for many years. He had been in and out of hospital for some time just before he died, but no matter how much his death had been expected, it was nevertheless a sad and sudden shock when it came for everyone who knew him.

On the day before he died, I vividly remember seeing the first swallows of the year. I recall noting that their return from warmer climates signalled the true beginning of spring in the Northern Hemisphere. I sensed their rather early arrival indicated we were going to have a very warm summer, and I remember thinking to myself that this was somehow a 'good' sign.

I spent much time in my garden that day, since my wife was visiting her family some miles away. The next morning, I received a phone call informing me of Harry's death.

Later on that same afternoon, I attended Harry's wake, where his close relatives were being comforted by a steady stream of visitors. As is the custom in a wake house in the region where I live, Harry's body lay in an open coffin. Along with other family members and mourners present, I was able to go quietly to the coffin to say a few personal words and prayers for the departed soul.

I remember privately thinking about all the time I had known Harry, and the genuine friendship he had shown me throughout this period. He had been a great lover of life, and had always been busy, inquisitive, conversational and involved.

I discovered that arrangements had been made for Harry's burial to take place in two days time. When I discussed this with my wife later that day, I realised I would not be able to attend the funeral due to work commitments. I therefore resolved to return to the wake house on the evening before the funeral in order to say one final, personal goodbye to Harry. For some peculiar reason, I felt strongly compelled to do this at the time.

That evening came, and I went back to the wake, this time accompanied by my wife. I recall we had to park some distance away from the house since there were so many other cars parked in the area.

My wife and I entered the house and spoke to a few people, before I finally approached Harry's open coffin to offer my private, parting prayers and thoughts. The room where the coffin was situated was quite filled with mourners by this stage.

What transpired at this point was the encounter that has transformed my life and existence to this day.

For some reason, when I looked into Harry's coffin this time, a sudden and stunning feeling entered my body. The feeling was, quite simply, that Harry was not there. Yes, there was a body, but Harry's true essence or soul had quite simply 'gone'.

I had never experienced this feeling from a dead body in my life before, not even when I had stood by this same body, in this same room, on the previous afternoon. I remember asking myself, *"Where's Harry? Where has he gone?"* I never got to finish the sentence or thoughts however, because I suddenly found myself in (what I can only describe as) a different time realm.

I felt as though I was standing inside some sort of 'time bubble', where time did not exist. No sound could be heard inside this bubble, but I was nevertheless able to look through the corner of my eye at other mourners going about their business in normal, earthly time sequence. I could see them talking, but couldn't hear the sounds they were making. I wasn't able to hear noises coming from anywhere else inside the house either. The other mourners all seemed to be in their own 'ordinary' time frame, which was much faster than the one I was now standing in. I began to panic and tried to turn in their direction, but all I could muster was a slight movement of my head to the left.

Another sensation of panic entered my body as it dawned on me that no one else in the room could see and feel what I was experiencing at that time. My wife was standing no more than a few feet away from me talking to someone, but it was as though any attempt on my part to communicate with her (or anyone else in the room) would be in vain for as long as I remained encapsulated inside this time bubble.

Something was happening to me, but I didn't know exactly what. All I knew was that time, from my perspective, had stopped, relative to how I was able to observe it outside the bubble through the movements of other people. I somehow realised I was completely detached from the other mourners and their experience of reality at that particular moment in time.

Then suddenly, as if someone flicked a switch, I found myself standing back in 'normal' time sequence. I felt inwardly shaken so much that my legs became slightly weak. The movements of the other mourners in the room now became much faster, and I was able to hear them very clearly. I stared at everyone for a few moments, wondering what had just happened. It became immediately obvious to me, however, that none of the other mourners were aware that anything unusual had occurred, since they all appeared to be talking and moving about as normal. I looked around me, feeling a little paranoid and self-conscious by this stage, and instinctively knew I had to leave the house immediately in order to get some fresh air – I just had to get out.

Something 'unearthly' had happened to me and I was in a daze because of it. But just exactly what had happened? The truth was, I simply didn't know.

I turned to my right and made an excuse to my wife for us to leave. When we arrived home, we sat quietly and watched a bit of television for a while. I felt slightly nervous and uneasy within myself, but tried to dismiss from my mind any other thoughts about what had occurred earlier that evening.

After an hour or so, we talked a little more about events at Harry's wake, and had a general conversation about who was there and what was said.

What we went on to eventually discuss, however, started a chain of events that has changed both our lives in a most profound and unforgettable way.

About ten minutes or so into one particular part of the conversation, my wife began to speak about how everybody would miss Harry and how sad the whole situation was. I would usually concur with these sentiments of loss and grieving, but I now began to feel a sudden, spontaneous sense of frustration and impatience in relation to what my wife was saying to me.

All of a sudden, a plethora of information and knowledge began to flow out of me. I said I didn't really understand why people were crying, because Harry wasn't there in his coffin. I told her that Harry was in a different place, and that he was very happy. My wife looked at me in a shocked and (understandably) confused manner and began to ask me where these ideas had so suddenly come from. What transpired during the remainder of the evening was a conversation for which neither of us could ever have prepared for or foreseen.

It revolved around my wife asking me a series of questions about what had happened to me beside Harry's coffin earlier that evening.

One question led to another, starting from the moment when I became aware on an earthly level that Harry's soul or essence had completely left his body.

I told her that I was encapsulated in some sort of 'time bubble', which had excluded me from everyone else in the house. I recounted how I was able to see everyone else in their 'normal' time frame, but wasn't able to hear them. I also informed her about how hard I had tried to get their attention. Most surprisingly, I was then able to describe what had happened to me inside the time bubble.

It became increasingly clear to me what must have happened as I had stood frozen for those few moments beside Harry's coffin. It was as though spiritual information had somehow been placed inside my mind, and now began to flow outwards, as though someone had turned on a tap to release it.

I found myself emphatically able to answer questions, whose meaning prior to this point in my life, I had hardly even contemplated or considered. Through answering these questions, I found to my disbelief that I was able to describe many things about life as it exists in the spiritual dimension after death.

I recalled that I was taken to a place I had never seen or been to before. I was held aloft in front of a huge red-brick wall. It was about twenty feet in height and had a curved top. This was the type of wall one would typically see around an enclosed or traditional walled garden. I was held at one particular point outside this wall, where I was unable to see to my left, but to my right-hand side, I could clearly see that the wall appeared to stretch into infinity.

In front of this wall, was a verge of translucent, green grass that extended approximately five feet out from it. Even though the wall was very high, I could still see above it. I was able to observe a beautiful blue sky containing just a few fluffy, symmetrical white clouds; it seemed as though they were there for purely aesthetic purposes.

Beyond the wall, the weather appeared to be very warm, as though it was a hot, sunny summer's day. The clouds did not move, indicating there was no wind, and I did not detect the possibility or existence of rain or any other weather turbulence. I do not recall sensing any particular smells either.

As I was held aloft in front of the wall, I began to hear murmurs and voices entering from my right-hand side across it. The wall was too high for me to see over, but I could clearly hear voices through it. I strongly sensed there was a multitude of people approaching the point beyond the wall where I was being held.

I somehow felt that these people had entered from some sort of tunnel or other type of entry point beyond the wall, and their voices became louder as they approached me on the opposite side of it. I could sense there were hundreds of people, all travelling slowly towards one particular point opposite me on the other side of the wall.

I couldn't hear exact or clear dialogue because there were so many people. I knew there were a lot of people, because a multitude of voices could be heard. It was a gentle babble of conversation, and everyone there seemed to be calm and collected. Now and then, in the midst of these voices, was a very familiar one: it was Harry's.

I could hear Harry talking to someone else across the wall. I recall sensing that everyone there spoke the same language, and I believe this was simply to ensure they could all understand what was being talked about.

As Harry approached the point nearest me on the other side of the wall, I strongly sensed that he and everybody else there were being directed by specifically appointed guides holding clipboards, which contained exact instructions about who should go where. It was as though Harry and the others were being given different jobs or tasks to do. As the people on the other side approached me, it seemed as though they then went off perpendicularly into the far distance. The image I sensed reminded me of hundreds of fans entering a football field from the players' tunnel.

I gauged that everyone on the other side of the wall was of a similar type, since I could not detect any difference in language, accent or design. I also sensed that everyone was of a light complexion, but I believe this was most probably due to the brightness there, rather than actual skin colour or tone.

There were no old people nor young children or babies, and I strongly sensed for some reason that everyone there was approximately thirty-three years old. This appeared to be irrespective of the age they had departed earth (Harry had been fifty-two at the time of his death). There was no disorder, and everyone there was very contented, happy and healthy. No-one appeared to have any earthly limitations or faults (such as hunger, pride or ego), since every soul was exactly the same as the next in every respect.

As I told my wife these things, I began to realise what exactly must have happened to me beside Harry's coffin earlier that night: I had been taken to a place where spirit souls were entering one of the many, many *energy levels* of Heaven.

As Harry and the other spirits across the wall entered from my right, I felt they must have infused me with their knowledge.

I had never before considered the existence of energy levels in Heaven, but from the knowledge I was now given, I somehow knew that the energy level Harry was on was just one of many.

I was 'told' that many spirits reside on each level, and do different jobs according to their specific role there. I discovered it is possible for spirits on higher energy levels to move down and visit spirits they know on the lower energy levels. However, I was also made aware that spirits on the lower energy levels cannot move into higher energy levels without the help of other spirits. I sensed that the spirits on the lower energy levels have to remain on their particular level for a period of time in order to acquire more spiritual energy. I was told the way a human conducts their life on earth, determines which level they enter the Spirit World upon their death.

I strongly sensed from across the wall that only pure friendships and relationships exist in the Spirit World, but not marriage. Every soul's essence seems to be part of everyone else's, and every spirit appears to be extremely happy. I detected this degree of contentedness from Harry, and I knew that under no circumstances would he ever want to return to the energy level of earth. I felt he now knew his happiness across the wall was eternal. Harry and the other spirits recognised that the energy level of the earth was much lower than that in their new realm of existence, and I therefore sensed hundreds of souls, eternally happy to be where they were.

I also gauged that all the spirits across the wall had entered from the same access point - irrespective of how or where they had died. It didn't seem to really matter how they had passed away on earth (whether this had been through a car accident or a heart attack), since they all entered in the same orderly manner. Whilst I wasn't able to see through the wall, I can't emphasise enough just how strongly I was able to sense what was going on across it.

Then, while all of this was happening, my attention was suddenly switched to my side of the wall.

Whoever (or whatever) brought me there, now focused my attention onto something else. I was turned in such a direction that I found myself looking down into the depths of space. I was able to see the earth far below on my right-hand side. It did not, however, appear as the beautiful blue and green planet, dashed with a covering of white clouds, which one would normally associate with photographs taken from space. Instead, the earth looked extremely grey and dull, as though it was sick or suffering in some way.

I strongly inferred this weakness had been caused by what humans had done to it, and I gained the strong impression the earth was ill in both a spiritual and physical manner. This knowledge was not taken from my own beliefs, but rather imparted to me as I stood by the wall looking down.

I was told, not in words, but through my senses, that this damage could be repaired if certain things happened. I gained the unmistakeable feeling that there is an absolute need for *love* and *prayer* if the earth is to be healed. I obtained the clear impression that this prayer must be for the whole earth and for everybody on it. I was also told there is a great need to pray for those who have passed away before us, and was informed that prayer should take the form of words and deeds. It should also dictate how people behave and think on earth.

I sensed the Spirit World (or Heaven) needs the love and prayer of people on earth, just as much as the earth needs the love and support of the Spirit World. I was told there is an urgent need to keep these two realms united and connected, and gained the distinct impression that everything is linked spiritually above and below. Finally, I sensed the earth will forfeit this spiritual connection if she does not change her current practices and behaviour.

I must stress at this point that although I had always believed in the idea of God and Heaven, and although I had occasionally prayed up to this point in my life, I had never felt so emphatic or passionate about the need for prayer, prior to this experience.

During my encounter at the wall, I was also given the opportunity to question the philosophy of 'Hell'. I was told that the concept of Hell (as we have come to understand it on earth) does not actually exist on any energy level beyond the realms of earth itself. Hell, in other words, does not exist in the traditional sense of evil spirits burning for eternity. It is created by humans on earth through their own greed and hatred, and through the self-inflicted misery and worry they bring upon themselves in their pursuit of material gain and their attempts to satisfy the ego.

Humans go through trials, tribulations and suffering everyday on earth, and if there is a Hell, then it relates to what happens here. The traditional notion of Hell, I gathered, is just a manifestation of old beliefs from various religious teachings. The spirits across the wall simply didn't have any awareness of an actual spiritual realm called 'Hell'.

I also gathered from this encounter that God is forever and always a *loving* God, so Hell only exists in the human mind because it was indoctrinated by old religious teachings. The philosophy from across the wall also dictates that a loving God does not need a Hell to put 'bad' or 'evil' spirits into. In reality, we create our own Hell through our personal behaviour and thoughts. It seems to me therefore, that Hell is simply life without God, and life without hope.

I must stress again that these concepts relating to Hell did not form part of my own philosophy or set of beliefs prior to this experience.

As I recounted this knowledge, I suddenly recalled how this encounter ended, and also remembered how I found myself standing back in 'normal time' once more beside Harry's coffin. As I recollected this, I became completely overwhelmed with emotion for the first time.

I recalled sensing that the spirits on the other side of the wall somehow gathered I was there. They all seemed to stop what they were doing, and turned around and 'stared' at me through the wall. The effect of hundreds of spirits looking at me with such intensity frightened me like I had never been frightened in my entire life. I couldn't see any spirit faces, but I could feel their spiritual intensity as though they were standing right beside me. I sensed they had discovered someone with a much lower energy level peering into their realm, and I somehow felt unworthy of being in their presence.

When whoever brought me to the wall realised I was frightened and in a panic, they instantly whisked me back to earth. It was at this point, I believe, that I exited the time bubble inside Harry's house, and once again became connected to life on a normal, earthly level.

After reflecting upon this information, I was very surprised at the level of knowledge I had obtained during my encounter. I clearly realised it did not stem from my personal, preconceived impressions of Heaven, since I had always envisaged this as a carefree place where spirits did what they wanted, when they wanted. I had never considered Heaven to be a place full of purpose, where serious spiritual work is still ongoing. Whilst I had always envisaged Heaven as being a happy place, I could never have imagined before this encounter just how rewarding, loving and fulfilling it actually is (or at least appeared to be on Harry's particular level). Indeed, I believe my sense of impatience at my wife's mourning and regret (the very thing that sparked my memory into action regarding all the information I describe here) came from the inherent knowledge that Harry was truly and eternally happy, and also from the strong belief that it would be completely unfair to deny or wish him away from the existence he now enjoyed.

Since having this encounter, I now believe that when we mourn for a departed loved one, we do so more for ourselves and our own sense of loss on earth, rather than for the person who has moved on. We should, on the contrary, feel delighted for them in their new state of being.

My experiences at the wall left me with a number of issues I had to address in respect of what I saw and was told there. I wondered firstly who or what had brought me to this realm. It appeared as though I had been very unexpectedly transported there when I asked about Harry's whereabouts.

When I recalled how the spirits across the wall reacted when they detected my earthly appearance and presence, I also questioned the exact nature of my relationship with them, and wondered why I had been taken to their realm.

The encounter also left me wondering about the significance of the red brick wall with its curved top and lush green grass. Again, I cannot be entirely sure about its purpose, but I have come to the conclusion (for now at least) that it was placed there simply as some sort of protective barrier between myself and the Spirit World beyond it.

Although I was not able to physically see through the wall, I was nevertheless able to obtain a very strong impression about certain things beyond it.

Firstly, I was able to clearly perceive that the climate there was warm and sunny, with temperatures pitched in the mid-twenties Celsius. It appears to me that this is a key characteristic of the environment in the Spirit World.

I was also able to note that the spirits beyond the wall were similar in age (approximately thirty-three years old), and were universally light in appearance. Of more consequence, perhaps, was the strong impression I gained of different energy levels in the Spirit World. I was given the distinct understanding that, depending upon the goodness or quality of life each human soul departs earth, then this very much determines the energy level they enter Heaven (or the Spirit World) upon their death. Similar souls enter similar energy levels (there are both higher and lower levels), and I had an unmistakable sense that those who do deliberate harm to others on earth, only do themselves harm when it comes to entering the spiritual realm of existence.

Finally, I must end this chapter by going back to the most important message I believe I was asked to take from this experience.

This concerns the connectedness, Godliness and 'Oneness' of everything in life - both below on earth, and above in Heaven. I cannot stress enough how much importance was placed on love and prayer during this encounter. I was emphatically told there is a need for interaction between life on earth, and life on a more Heavenly or spiritual level.

I feel in many respects unqualified and humble imparting this knowledge, but I nevertheless believe it is the key to understanding all that I experienced on this occasion.

Indeed, much of what I discovered here was reaffirmed during a further series of encounters in the immediate six-month period following this one.

Chapter 4

The Park

During this vision, I met a man who died only a week or so prior to my actual encounter with him.

The encounter took place in September 2006, and it was rather brief in duration; it lasted only ten minutes.

I hadn't know the man I met in the encounter during his lifetime on earth, and in fact I had only ever seen a single photograph of him - the one attached to the newspaper article reporting on his untimely death. His passing captured my thoughts for a number of reasons, but mainly because of its very sudden and tragic nature. He had died at the age of nineteen due to a very unexpected and short illness.

On the evening this vision occurred, I was reflecting almost casually to myself about how I would love to be able to tell the deceased man's family not to despair, in the belief their son and brother was safely positioned in a happier and higher realm – knowledge so clearly imparted to me as I had stood outside *The Wall* only months previously.

Then, while having dinner that evening, all the emotions and feelings I encountered at *The Wall* came flooding back to me.

I felt a tremendous emotional pressure from 'above', which I instinctively knew came from another dimension. This sensation was accompanied by a most peculiar smell, which reminded me of a room containing old, musty books that had not been opened for a very long time. The odour was extremely intense in nature, and when I breathed in through my nose, it felt as though a heavy vapour or mist was infusing my brain, just as one would observe a heavy, dense fog slowly weaving through an apple orchard in autumn.

Suddenly, an image materialised in front of me, just above the level of my head, and slightly to my right. It appeared initially as a rather blurred vision of the half torso of (what appeared to be) a young man. The image had soft, whitish edges, which filtered in and out of my reality: after a few seconds, it eventually became fully focused.

The size of the image became larger, and I could now see a more distinct vision incorporating all of the young man. He bent over and stared searchingly and inquisitively into my eyes, as though he was looking into a two-way mirror that had a small light behind it.

I immediately sensed from the image before me that the young man was appearing from some spiritual realm above and beyond the earth. Although he was definitely on a higher energy level than earth, I felt he was not, however, as elevated as the spirits I had encountered behind

The Wall. I wondered what the significance of this was, and questioned why the atmosphere seemed a little heavier on this occasion. I must say this unsettled me slightly at the time.

In the vision, the young man appeared to be approximately thirty years old. He had a tanned complexion and slightly rugged appearance. He looked like he had been exposed to the sun for some time, and he appeared to be very tired. He had distinctive, cropped, light red hair, and I was clearly able to see his attire. The young man wore an aquamarine, v-necked sweater made from fine wool, as well as a pair of modern-day, light-blue jeans, but I could not see any kind of footwear.

Whilst still stooping over slightly, the young man stared at me inquisitively for a second time, but he now attempted to focus more clearly upon me.

The young man began to squint, and I could see frustration in his facial expression. His posture began to stiffen, adding to this look of discomfort.

Although he appeared to be looking at me, I was now unsure as to whether the young man could actually see me, or perhaps (I thought) he simply realised he had not found what he was looking for.

I somehow sensed the young had been travelling or searching for some time, and he appeared to be tired from his exposure to the heat in his new, spiritual realm of existence.

As I sat absorbing all of this, I suddenly became frozen to the spot. I now realised I recognised this man from the black and white photograph I had seen only a week or so earlier. The reason I had not immediately made this connection was due to the age of the man as he appeared during this encounter. He was approximately thirty years old as I saw him in front of me now, but in the photograph he had been the age he was when he died – nineteen. I was fully confident, however, that the man in my vision and the one in the photograph were one and the same.

As the vision played out in front of me, the young man's frustration appeared to increase until he decided to leave with a small shrug of his shoulders. It was as though he had not found what he was searching for. He turned his back on me and walked away several metres. As he moved further into the distance, I noticed that his shoulders were somewhat rounded, and also that he stooped slightly to his right-hand side. I again perceived this to be an indication of his weariness. He momentarily paused and glanced over his left shoulder towards me once more, but this time with quite a profound look of disappointment.

As he continued to walk further away from me, the image began to widen and I was able to perceive other bits and pieces I hadn't seen before.

I noticed it was late evening (or even twilight) where the young man was, since the light there was fading to such an extent that I could make out shadowy background objects in the image.

The young man then started to move towards two large, silhouetted objects that resembled very tall trees. I sensed he was walking on grass - as though he was in some sort of park. I again felt he was lost, because it seemed as though he didn't really know where he was going. He appeared to be searching for something (like a gate or doorway) to take him out of this park. The overwhelming impression I gained of the young man's disposition and mood at this time was certainly not as contented or relaxed as Harry's had been at *The Wall*. I wondered why this was the case, and return to consider this issue later in the book.

The last I saw of the young man was when he walked away from me so far that he simply faded into the farthest edges of the vision in front of me. As he disappeared, the image began to slowly collapse, until everything eventually merged back into my reality.

As I took some time to compose myself once the vision had passed, I realised that all I had witnessed had taken no more than ten minutes of earthly time. Much more time appeared to have lapsed within the image itself, however. Time, in the young man's realm, appeared to be much slower and more concentrated than time in my reality. The main reason I say this is because of the movements of the young man himself. I would describe these as being much slower and more intense than the movement or speed of events in 'real time', or time as it appears on earth. If I could compare it to anything, then I would say it reminded me of watching an old cine-film movie slowed down to about two-thirds speed. Time *did* however exist in *The Park*, unlike my encounter at *The Wall* and with the *Little Boy*, when I experienced a definite feeling of *timelessness*.

I also recognised that the images I saw during this encounter appeared and emerged from my right of vision, similar to how they did during most of my other encounters.

I likewise gained the definite impression of a warm climate from this encounter (due to the young man's attire and tanned complexion), and this also correlated with the warm atmosphere I sensed during my encounter at *The Wall*.

The age of the person in this vision was approximately ten years more than he had been on earth (thirty years old instead of nineteen), and I also questioned why this was the case.

Finally, I asked myself what this young man was searching for, and wondered why he didn't appear as contented as the spirits across *The Wall*. This was the most bothering thing about this particular encounter for me. I felt I wanted this young man to be elsewhere in the Spirit World, and wondered who or what was holding him back from attaining a lighter and happier state of being.

After this encounter, I began to recognise that something profound was happening to me, and realised these were not one-off experiences.

Indeed, it was not long before I had a further encounter with the Spirit World. I describe it in detail in the next chapter.

Chapter 5

The Room

I experienced another encounter exactly a week after that with the young man. Nothing, however, could have prepared me for what I saw and felt on this occasion.

On Monday 2nd October 2006, a very old acquaintance of my father's appeared to me as a spirit entity. I had never met this man, since he had died some years before I was actually born, and I had only ever seen his image in photographs.

I sensed I was going to have another spiritual encounter because I felt an extremely strong connection with the Spirit World on the Saturday prior to it. These spiritual links felt so strong on one particular occasion that day, I had to ask the spirits to leave me alone. I simply didn't feel emotionally strong enough to cope with their overwhelming strength of presence and energy, and I did my best during the remainder of the weekend to ignore their attempts to make contact with me.

By Monday, however, I knew these attempts would be in vain. I was not exactly sure about *who* was trying to contact me, although I admit that a number of images, faces and names fleeted in and out of my mind during this time. One of these was later to become very significant.

The strong smell I previously experienced with the young man in *The Park* was by now so intense, it pervaded all my senses and emotions. In addition to this, I felt an immense pressure from above, but this time the sensation was more pronounced than ever. I felt very sure that whoever this spirit was trying to contact me, they were coming from a much higher energy level than I had ever experienced before.

By the time I returned home from work that Monday evening, I knew something was imminent. I went to have my tea as usual just after

5.30 p.m. - but I was so overwhelmed emotionally by this stage, my wife began to enquire about who I believed was trying to contact me.

She managed by chance to mention three possible spirit candidates, whose images I had fleetingly glimpsed during the course of the previous weekend. I cannot explain why these particular deceased souls had entered my thoughts at this time, except to say I was by now intensely aware of the existence of a Spirit World, and was fully awake to the idea that we are all deeply connected to life on that other level.

It was upon mentioning the third name (my father's old acquaintance) that the whole experience finally culminated. I could not, however, have imagined in a thousand years what I was about to see and experience. Then the vision began.

The encounter opened in the same way as that with *The Park* had, but this time the images appeared much closer to my face. Once again, they emerged from my right-hand side perspective, just above the level of my head. I didn't see my father's acquaintance at first, but what I did see unsettled me to the extent that I became almost frightened.

In front of me, was an entity trying to force its face into my line of vision. It did this several times. It took me a while to fully absorb what I was looking at, without at first questioning my own sanity. In fact, the entity I saw was so far removed from anything I had ever realistically contemplated prior to this point in my life, I still feel somewhat strange and surreal speaking about it. I am fully confident, however, about everything I witnessed on this occasion.

The entity vying for my attention was an adult, male elf. It was approximately three to four feet in height, was clean-shaven and had very dark hair and eyebrows. The elf's forehead protruded slightly from its large, elongated head - a head much larger in proportion to any human being's. Its face had very distinctive features: A pointed, downward-curving nose, met a huge protruding chin, which curved sharply upwards. The elf had an extremely sallow, swarthy-looking complexion, dark eyes and a very thin mouth. Its ears were rather small in proportion to its large, elongated head.

As the vision opened up further, I was now able to watch the elf manoeuvre itself back towards a group of similar-looking entities.

The elves in this awaiting group were uniform in appearance. They each wore dark green, three-quarter length pants, and they were bare-footed. They didn't wear any shirts or tops, and therefore exposed ashen-looking, smooth skin on their torsos. They were all very toned. The group consisted of about six or seven elves, but most captivatingly, they were all dancing in a circle.

The dynamics of this dance were fascinating; it resembled no dance routine I had ever witnessed before. I would best describe it as a three-dimensional dance, whose origin and rhythm stemmed from Nature itself. It was magical, exquisite, thrilling and enchanting all at the same time. The movements of the dance appeared to be very mathematical and coordinated, as though they were governed by some natural phenomenon or the laws of Nature.

The elves danced quickly in a simple circle. Individually, they moved up and down in some sort of sine-wave fashion, and with a very precise, coordinated, three-dimensional figure of eight motion. As they danced, their arms moved in conjunction with their bodies. On the upward movement of the sine-curve, the elves moved deliberately slowly and perfectly coordinated together. However, on the downward motion they accelerated, and they really emphasised this quicker movement, with their bodies, arms and heads in synchronous motion. Another curious thing I noticed was that as the elves danced in their circle, they appeared to be bent over by about forty-five degrees. They also appeared to be completely malleable, such was the degree of flexibility and ease of movement their bodies displayed.

This dance must have been created and synchronised by Nature itself, because no human could ever possibly mimic what I witnessed. Once the dance started, it was as though someone hit a repeat button. The elves didn't stop dancing, nor did they make the slightest mistake in their never-ending loop routine; the motion simply repeated and started again.

Now I began to see further into the vision than before. Standing in the background, was a man who was approximately sixty years old. I recognised who he was from photographs I had seen before. It was undoubtedly my father's old friend, who was affectionately known as 'Grandpa Joe' during his life on earth.

He was smiling at me, sort of chuckling really. He stood tall and elegant with his hands down by his blue trousers. He had a well-defined, rounded face and rather bushy eyebrows, which were slightly darker than his remaining grey hair. He was tanned by the sun and wore a white terylene T-shirt (the type which I believe was quite common during the 1970s). The T-shirt was short-sleeved and had a white collar with a thin, dark blue stripe inset from its edge. Each sleeve was also trimmed with a thin, dark blue stripe, and appeared to have some sort of elastic around it – I suppose to keep the sleeve tight around the arm muscle.

Grandpa Joe was balding on top, but had a muscular, toned, and well-defined physique. This made him look very fit, even for a man whose age I guessed was about sixty in this vision.

I gained the impression he had somehow 'entered' this space from some place or realm beyond where I was able to see in my vision. It was as though he had accessed a separate room on another energy level, through which he was now able to make a connection with me on earth. I somehow sensed he had entered this room from a much higher energy level than the one I was encountering in my vision.

The Room was empty except for the presence of Grandpa Joe and the elves. It was brilliant white in colour, and appeared to be warm in temperature.

The energy the elves and Grandpa Joe brought with them almost overwhelmed me both emotionally and physically. Grandpa Joe stood smiling in the background, while the elves continued dancing in the foreground. I sensed it was he who controlled the elves, because they appeared to be quite simply at his beck-and-call.

I gained a strong impression of Grandpa Joe's personality through this vision, despite never having met him in life. He appeared to have a keen sense of fun, or even mischief, and I felt he definitely knew I was the son of his old friend - he appeared to be simply dropping by to say "Hello" to me.

As the encounter unfolded, my wife was sitting across the table from me. She enquired as to what was going on, but try as I did to let her know what was happening, my emotions were simply too overwhelming for me to speak. Attempting to concentrate on a band of dancing elves and a high-energy spirit was enough for me to take on board at this time!

I must say I found it difficult to look at Grandpa Joe directly. I had to put my head down and look away from his direct gaze several times, and I think this caused him some curiosity. Due to my inability to make direct visual contact with him, Grandpa Joe appeared to become slightly bemused and frustrated with me. I don't believe he understood my earthly sense of inadequacy, or my inability to fully compose myself at this time. I now began to sense he had enough of this meeting, and felt disinclined to continue with it further. I think he became frustrated because I was not experienced enough to deal with his energy or the images he was showing me at this time.

In hindsight, I believe Grandpa Joe wanted to communicate with me, but since I wasn't able deal with the situation in hand, a more productive meeting couldn't take place. I felt on reflection afterwards that I had subconsciously invited him to meet me by thinking about him. However, when he appeared to me, or accepted my invitation to meet him, I somehow reneged on the meeting from his perspective.

As a direct result of this, he turned his head away from me, and began to move off to the right-hand side of the room. It seemed as though he was now waiting for something or somebody to remove him from this space. The elves as an entire group went over to join him, as though they were sheepdogs subserviently following their master's lead.

The vision then started to collapse, and Grandpa Joe and his elves began to disappear from view. I thought the encounter had ended, but I was wrong.

After several minutes, Grandpa Joe appeared again, still standing on the same spot with the elves dancing in the foreground. He turned around and focused on me, but then quickly looked away again. The vision faded away for a second time, and this happened twice more before it finally ended.

When I composed myself after a few moments, I couldn't believe how much time had passed by in the 'real' world. The encounter had started at around 5.45 p.m. and didn't finish until 7.10 p.m. I had literally been taken away from my own reality for nearly an hour and twenty-five minutes. What was I to make of what had just happened?

The first thing I found myself questioning after this encounter was the existence and purpose of Grandpa Joe's elves. They appeared to be in total deference to him. He was their master and they were totally obedient to him. They were his constant companions, and went wherever he went. The elves were obviously not human in any shape or form, and they appeared to exist only for the purpose of serving Grandpa Joe, or perhaps even for his amusement. They appeared to be an integral part of his character, and it seemed (to me) as though they had once been with him on earth, and were now with him in his spiritual life.

I strongly felt *The Room* was off some sort of corridor, which spirits were permitted to enter in order to communicate with people from earth. It was also interesting to note that Grandpa Joe could not leave this room until he was either allowed to, or until his time had somehow been used up.

Once again, the vision appeared and emerged from my right-hand side perspective, and there were many other aspects of this encounter that correlated with those at *The Wall* and *The Park*.

Firstly, I sensed the existence of different spiritual energy levels during this encounter. I felt the energy brought by Grandpa Joe on this occasion was higher, stronger and more intense than Harry's at *The Wall*, but especially more so than the young man's in *The Park*. The energy each of these spirit entities brought, however, was still much greater than mine on earth, and I was therefore left to ponder the significance and meaning of these energy levels.

Grandpa Joe appeared as a man in his early sixties in this vision, but he had been eighty-six years old when he passed away. Indeed, the only images I had ever seen of him were in photographs taken of him at this older age (and when he was formally dressed in a suit and tie), so I therefore wondered why these differences in age and appearance existed.

During this encounter, I gained the distinct impression of a sunny and warm climate, given Grandpa Joe's attire and sun-tanned skin.

Although I didn't get the feeling this was an overly oppressive or uncomfortably hot environment, I would nevertheless say that temperatures in the Spirit World were pitched somewhere in the mid-twenties Celsius.

From the three visions at *The Wall, The Park* and on this occasion, I didn't get the impression that this climate changed much, and I therefore suspect it remains pretty much constant at this temperature all of the time. In fact, the only time I sensed a hint of discomfort and overheating in the spiritual realms was during my encounter with the young man in *The Park*. However, I do have an idea as to why the climate differed on this particular occasion, and I return to this issue later in the book.

As for the age of the spirits who appeared to me during my encounters, I was able to make a number of observations. Grandpa Joe came to me as a youthful man in his early sixties, even though he had died on this earth as a man in his mid-eighties. The young man in *The Park* appeared to be approximately thirty years of age, despite having died at the age of nineteen. Although I didn't physically see Harry or the others across *The Wall*, I gained the distinct impression of a gathering of young adults in their early thirties (from sensing their movements and hearing the sound of their voices). Harry, however, had died at the age of fifty-two. What, I asked myself, was the significance of these ages, and why did the spirits all appear either younger or older than when they had departed earth? I address these points in the concluding chapters of the book.

Finally, one particular thing struck me about the encounter with Grandpa Joe, and this was the vivid impression I was given of his personality and essence. It is this vision that makes me feel equipped to note something specific about life beyond.

I had never met Grandpa Joe in life. Although I had heard him spoken of occasionally by my family, I genuinely did not have a clear idea about who he was before this encounter, other than what his physical appearance was from the few photographs I had seen.

When I privately recounted this vision to someone who had once been close to Grandpa Joe, they immediately smiled in clear recognition of the man they had known personally on earth. His spirit or essence was essentially the same above as it had been below. The clear sense of fun and playful mischievousness I gauged from this vision was in accordance with stories I began to be told about Grandpa Joe's ways and attitudes on earth.

Perhaps most curious of all was Grandpa Joe's relationship and connection to the unforgettable and remarkable group of elves. Their striking appearance, enigmatic dance and mischievous mannerisms seemed to so closely reflect the essence of Grandpa Joe himself. He had a definite master-servant relationship with them, and they were completely at his beck-and-call. Grandpa Joe had, however, a definite fondness and affection for the elves, and a strong affinity with them. He was 'One' with their natural life force, and they were 'One' with his.

These elves were truly magnificent entities. In fact, despite my own initial reservations, I realised they were wonderful beings and possessed no negative or harmful energy whatsoever.

Whilst I had never ruled out the existence of other spiritual life-forms prior to this encounter, I need to emphasise my initial astonishment and shock at the mythological or 'fairytale' aspect of this vision. I am absolutely definite, however, about everything I saw and experienced on this occasion.

Finally, I must before I end this chapter mention another thing I came to know about Grandpa Joe's earlier life on earth. I discovered he had worked as a cobbler for many years during his adulthood.

This aspect stretched my old beliefs and attitudes about the Spirit World even further.

Perhaps it is only a coincidence, but I am sure most people have heard the (Brothers Grimm) story of "The Elves and The Shoemaker"...

Chapter 6

The Real Moon Fairy

I was conscious after my encounters at *The Wall, The Park* and *The Room* that something quite profound was occurring in my life.

At times, I do admit I felt somewhat curious and even perplexed as to why these things were happening, and wondered where, if anywhere, they were leading me.

After my encounter with Grandpa Joe, I wondered if there would be any more spiritual experiences. I did not automatically *expect* anything else to happen to me, but to my great pleasure, other visions did occur.

The first of these took place on Monday 23rd October, exactly three weeks after my encounter with Grandpa Joe.

The experience I speak about in this chapter is very different to those I had at *The Wall*, *The Park* or *The Room*. It was, however, possibly the most spiritually rewarding of all my experiences to date.

During this encounter, I met with a genuinely pure, light being. This entity was a spirit of Nature, or '*deva*'.

I will describe what happened on this occasion by firstly explaining how I believe the experience came about. In order to do this, I feel I need to comment upon the relationship I have had with Nature and the Cosmos since I was a very young child. This explanation will hopefully enable others to fully appreciate the deeper meaning of the encounter.

As a young boy, I always had a genuine fascination with Nature. I could easily sit for hours contemplating the trees, grass, flowers, birds and sky in all their beauty. Without hopefully sounding crass or clichéd, I would say I felt somehow 'connected' with their life and energy. I was especially captivated by all things astronomical, and by the vastness and richness of the universe in which I lived. I truly sensed as a child (and as I became an adult) the essential 'Oneness' of life, and constantly pondered the nature of my own existence in relation to all of these things.

I sensed that everything in Nature was truly alive and 'at One', to the extent that I always embraced the possibility of different life forms (this seemed to be confirmed through my extraordinary vision of Grandpa Joe and his elves). It was from this deeply felt conviction, I believe, that the vision I go on to describe here manifested.

During the weekend prior to Monday 23rd October, I had been tending to some plants in my garden. This garden was of particular pride to me, since I had planted it from new only a year previously, and I felt I had created and shaped it. In one particular part of the garden, I had planted some plants and flowers I had always considered 'magical'. The plants in question were a combination of forget-me-not, hosta, primula, a tree fern (the type *Dicksonia Antarctica*) and, believe it or not, a gooseberry bush!

That part of the garden is in a shady position, and it was planted to merge comfortably with the large established trees that bordered it.

This cool and shady area felt very special to me, and the plants I chose for it were selected deliberately to create a kind of enchanted forest feel. I loved this place the most when gushes of sunbeams could be seen penetrating the trees and plants, making this special corner sparkle like the diamond ring effect of a total eclipse of the sun.

That weekend was fair in terms of weather, and I was tending to some things in the garden. Even though it was October, the plants were in a very healthy condition, with some of them still in flower. I knelt down beside the plants to lift some fallen leaves and felt an amazing peacefulness surround me. I knew this little corner of my garden was very special. I instinctively believed it was an enchanted place, and somehow sensed it was inhabited by living entities that protected it. I smiled amusedly at this thought, and became very touched by the emotions I felt at this time. Then, as a complete act of spontaneity, arising directly from my feeling of 'Oneness' with Nature, I began to compose some verse in my mind to capture what I was experiencing and thinking. I recall the verse as going something like this:

I know I cannot see you

But I know that you are there

I know I may never see you

But I know that you are there

Dancing on Forget-me-nots

Skipping 'cross the ferns

I know I cannot see you

But I know that you are there

I wasn't just talking to the plants, but in a childish and playful way, I was also talking to their inhabitants - whoever they were! I then left the garden feeling happy, peaceful and contented, and thought nothing more of this incident.

On Sunday evening, I went to bed as usual and slept. I awoke at about 3.00a.m. and stared out of the window, which was positioned to the right of my bed. The curtains were half-drawn as I always allow some natural light into the room at night-time.

As I lay awake looking up at the window, I spotted Orion in its fullest glory, with its two main stars, Betelgeuse and Rigel, shining brightly at its two opposite corners. Diagonally down from Orion's belt was the brilliant Sirius (the 'Dog Star'), shining with magnificent glory, like some beacon on a dark autumn night.

I remember wondering whether I should go downstairs and get a drink (as I was slightly thirsty), but I just lay on looking at the stars, whose names I had known since my childhood fascination with them had begun years ago. By this time I was probably awake for at least thirty minutes.

Then, the most amazing and wonderful thing happened right before my eyes.

Through one of the window panes jetted two parallel beams of white light. As I lay in bed, they entered on my right-hand side from the direction of the window. Just before they reached me, the parallel beams of light separated in a parabolic fashion in opposite directions, and stopped about three feet up and to my left. What transpired then totally astonished me. The two beams morphed into a tiny angel with an accompanying Orb.

I immediately knew that both the little angel and its companion Orb brought with them a sense of peacefulness, awe and amazement. I fondly came to refer to the main spirit entity (the angel) as 'The Real Moon Fairy'.

This angel pulsated like a stroboscope at very high frequency. She was about three or four inches in height, and the little Orb was only slightly smaller in diameter. Her face had no eyes or mouth as we normally recognise them, but there were dark indentations in the usual eye and mouth positions. She had a slight bump for a nose, which was just visible, but I could not perceive any ears, nor could I discern any hands, arms or feet.

As I looked at her face, I couldn't help thinking it resembled the faces on the statues on Easter Island in the Pacific Ocean, which I had seen many times in pictures and documentaries.

The Moon Fairy's entire body pulsated with a 'washing powder white' colour. This wasn't a pure white tone, but rather contained small, silvery-grey flecks, thus resulting in a sort of dappled effect.

She was wearing some sort of robe or gown, which was integrated into, or acted like her body. The robe had no visible connections to her neck or face, and it was as though her body and head were wholly conjoined.

The Moon Fairy's body pulsated at a very, very rapid frequency. Even more significant than this, however, were her wings, which protruded vertically from the top of her shoulders. They were about one quarter the length of the Moon Fairy, and they pulsated much faster than the rest of her body. Neither her wings nor her body had any hair, and she appeared to be completely smooth all over.

The Orb emitted small, pulsating lights: they were the same colour as the Moon Fairy's face and body, and they rotated in a random, erratic, multi-directional manner. I didn't discern any pattern to their pulsation, but a most amazing thing happened each time a little light pulsed on and off. As they pulsed *on*, I could see the tiny faces of unknown entities emerging. These entities popped their heads up now and again to look at me. I somehow sensed they were very young and playful spirits, and I was very curious about their purpose and significance.

As I looked on, it appeared as though the Moon Fairy was staring at me directly, but then she turned towards the entities within the Orb and seemed to gesture and encourage them to come out and have a look themselves. When she motioned towards them, she did not have a neck to turn, but rather moved her whole body as a complete object. She hovered and turned much in the same way a humming bird would when it searches for nectar inside a tropical flower.

The Moon Fairy did this several times, beckoning to the entities within the Orb to emerge and snatch a look at me. I sensed that she was instructing them to look at a human, as though I was some sort of peculiar or odd being. In a way, I felt as though I was the strange or alien entity on this occasion, and not they!

I thought to myself just how beautiful this little angel hovering beside me was, and smiled from the peaceful and calm aura she brought with her. I watched for about four or five minutes, and then outstretched my left hand towards them in a gesture of friendliness. This seemed to slightly startle the Moon Fairy because she began to vibrate her wings a little faster. I kept on smiling to myself, thinking what a wonderful sight this was to witness and behold.

Then suddenly, as quickly as they had materialised, the Moon Fairy and her Orb disappeared into the two beams of light, and were gone. They did not exit the window in the same way they had entered, but simply melted into the starlight and moonlight beaming through the bedroom window.

What was I to make of what had just happened? Was I dreaming? I lay on the bed and realised I was totally and absolutely wide awake: this was definitely not a dream.

Afterwards, I was able to make a number of observations based on my encounter with the

Moon Fairy and her orb. Although I refer to the Moon Fairy as a female entity, *she* was however completely androgynous. I only find myself alluding to a 'she', due to the soft and feminine aura she brought with her. The Moon Fairy was by no means a product of fairytale, nor was she a fanciful figment of my imagination.

I felt that she either controlled or acted as an adult figure to the little entities contained within the Orb. It was she who gestured to them to be brave and pop their tiny heads out to have a look at me.

The beams of pure, brilliant white light the Moon Fairy and Orb used to enter my bedroom were like wisps of light. They were not two fixed, solid beams as one would normally see in a searchlight, but were slightly more diffuse in nature.

Once the Moon Fairy exited with her Orb, I began to question where she had arrived from, and indeed, where it was she had returned to. It was at this stage that I made the connection with the magical, shady part of the garden outside my bedroom window – the place I had felt so spiritually connected to earlier that weekend.

I remembered my poem to the fairies. I felt that because I had shown my *true faith* in their presence in the garden, they had reciprocated this faith by appearing to me. I also believe they came in order to confirm the existence of *angels* and *fairies*.

But who exactly was the Moon Fairy? She was, I believe, an angel, albeit a very tiny one. She was fairy-like in appearance, but I truly sensed that she was an angel of Nature, whose role it was to protect the plants and flowers in her charge. I have no doubt that she emanated from the section of garden I had so strongly and spiritually connected to earlier that weekend.

The *Moon Fairy* wasn't like any angel I had ever seen before in photographs or pictures, nor was she human in form (like the *Little Boy*). She was the only entity I met who had wings, and I therefore believe she is a pure angel of Nature, or '*deva*'. I would not describe her as a spirit, since spirits (to me) signify that they were incarnate at some point in time, and she had certainly never been incarnate. The Moon Fairy brought with her a sense of peacefulness, but in a different way than the *Little Boy* had.

I believe very strongly that the key to understanding why this encounter took place lies in the fact that I demonstrated true faith in the existence of nature spirit entities.

Indeed, I believe my faith in the Spirit World as a whole made all my encounters possible.

———————

I had intended at this point in the book to write my concluding chapters. This was in the belief that my encounter with the Moon Fairy would possibly be the last of my spiritual experiences.

Whilst in the process of writing, however, I experienced another encounter, but initially hesitated about including its details in the book. On reflection, I feel strongly compelled to write about this particular encounter nonetheless, mainly because of a remarkable discovery I made in respect of its events a short time after it happened. I also want to describe it because of its very close connections to the Moon Fairy, as well as its links to the elves in *The Room*.

This most recent vision has further confirmed my faith in the world of nature spirits, and in the spiritual life of this planet as a whole.

Chapter 7

The Party

The event in this chapter occurred, I believe, as a direct sequel to my encounter with the *Moon Fairy*. I found myself questioning this event's meaning and substance even more than I had my other visions, however, mainly because of an extraordinary discovery I subsequently made in relation to its events and characters.

It was the morning of Friday 2nd February 2007, and the full moon was rising in the night sky. I felt particularly drawn to this full moon for some reason, but didn't really know why at the time. There was nothing obvious to suggest that this full moon was different to any other, but I nevertheless felt very connected to it.

Nothing of note occurred on the evening prior to this particular encounter. I came home from work and settled in for a quiet night watching some television. I noticed how the moon that night was particularly bright, with its millions of moonbeams lighting up everything in their path. I remarked to myself how beautiful it looked, and then simply went to bed and thought no more about it.

At approximately 3.00 a.m. I woke up to get a drink of water. In the far distance, through the cold frosty air, I could hear loud voices. I went over to the window and looked out across my back garden towards the direction of these noises. In the distance, I could see three people walking up the road, probably coming home from having a night out somewhere. They were very easy to see because by now the moon was very high in the night sky, and everything outside radiated with a warm, greenish-blue colour.

My back garden was clearly visible since the moonlight was illuminating everything in very clear detail. It was quite cold, so I had my drink and went straight back to bed.

I woke up again and looked at the time on my watch. It was by now just after 5.30 a.m. My attention was drawn once more to the garden, because it seemed so bright outside on this cold, February morning. I got out of bed quietly and walked over to the window.

As I got closer to it, I immediately noticed a small, three-leaved plant positioned on the inside of the windowsill. The light of the full moon was illuminating it, and to my astonishment, I noticed clearly how two of its three leaves were vibrating. This vibration was random, and had no particular pattern or rhythm associated with its movements.

I stared more closely now at the two vibrating leaves, which were clearly bouncing up and down under the beams of moonlight. The third leaf was not in direct moonlight and was not vibrating at all. I felt the radiator underneath the windowsill with my hand to check if its rising heat was causing the leaves to move; it was completely cold, since it had been turned off several hours previously.

I tried to discern any other logical reason as to why these leaves might be moving up and down, but simply couldn't find any.

I was drawn once more to the window and felt a strong urge to peer down into the garden below. When I looked, I became slightly startled at what I now beheld there.

I observed trails of movement through the (by now) very cold, frosty mist sitting over the garden. They reminded me of trails left in the wake of an aircraft high up in the cold atmosphere on a clear day. These trails were zipping about the garden in all directions and followed no set pattern.

Just as surely as I had been infused with knowledge and images at *The Wall*, I now found myself instinctively receiving a clear impression about what was happening outside beneath my window.

I could sense hundreds of playful voices coming from the garden. These voices seemed to be those of children and grown-ups alike, with the children's voices providing the most animated cheers and shouts of joy.

Suddenly, as my senses grew stronger, I recognised and understood just exactly what was going on outside. I strongly perceived a multitude of spirit entities in the garden below. These entities appeared to be from the far corners of the world of Nature itself.

The voices I heard included those of small fairies, who were sliding down the beams of moonlight onto the frozen blades of grass and plants in the garden beneath. They were playing everywhere in the garden - running, dancing, skipping and sliding. It reminded me of a group of children having great fun in an adventure playground. I could sense that these little fairies moved quite quickly from place to place, and they left small distinct trails behind them. It was as though they were celebrating or having a party. These fairies, or spirits, reminded me of the tiny entities that had emerged from within the *Moon Fairy's* Orb some months previously.

The fairies weren't the only entities in the garden that night, however, nor were they the most senior in importance or status.

Overlooking the various types of little fairy, were older and larger ones. I sensed for some reason that they were called *The Elders*, and they stood much taller and straighter than any other entity in the garden. They appeared to have a supervisory role, as though they were overseeing children in a playground situation. I sensed that they were standing at strategic points in the garden. They were making sure that while everyone was having fun, they were also safe and accounted for.

The Elders were tall and slender in appearance and were approximately four feet in height. They wore long robes that were milk-chocolate brown in colour and went all the way down to their feet. They had long faces and dark hair, which was tightly slicked back off their foreheads. I would say that their faces were more animal-like than they were human, albeit that they appeared to be very smooth in appearance. Their skin was very taut and their faces were elongated, as though they had been stretched during some sort of cosmetic procedure. The Elders also had eyes, a nose, a mouth and ears. Their features were not, however, as pointed or curved as those of the elves during my encounter with Grandpa Joe.

As the little ones played on, the Elders watched with their arms folded, as though they were in some sort of parental role. They stood smiling, as the tiny spirits danced, skipped and had their fun.

I then sensed other fairy-like entities I hadn't noticed before. For some reason, however, I didn't feel inclined to search these particular spirits out in my mind's eye. I sensed that I wouldn't be ready for or comfortable with what I would see if I did. Wisdom took over, and I stepped back slightly from the window, and stood behind one of the curtains. From this position, I could still clearly see the two leaves of the plant in the windowsill vibrating. I now knew that the little fairies, who were sliding down the moonlight beams from outside in the garden, were the cause of this vibration.

I glanced out of the window one more time, but withdrew again quite quickly because I somehow instinctively felt that I should not disturb the Elders, whom I strongly sensed were having some sort of private or ritualistic celebration in the garden below. I did not feel it was my place to intrude on this occasion any further.

I went back to bed, glancing one more time at the vibrating leaves of the plant in the windowsill. I wondered why all of these fairies and Elders were having this huge celebration in my back garden. I deeply sensed that it must be something to do with the full moon, but didn't truly understand what its real significance was at that time.

I also wondered if this party was a one-off event, or whether in fact this sort of occurrence happened all of the time, unbeknown to me. It was as though I was sensing the flow of Nature's numerous energy forces from deep within the earth on this occasion.

I fell asleep contented, knowing that everyone in the garden was having a wonderful time. I was also very happy since I felt that this encounter was confirmation of sorts that the *Moon Fairy* and her Orb had been real entities. I somehow sensed that they too were in the garden at this time, partaking in these moonlight festivities.

The next morning, I recalled everything that had happened the previous night in my garden, and I thought about the entities that had their huge party under the light of the full moon.

Later on that evening, purely by chance, I happened to look at a diary I had received as a Christmas present. I was casually browsing through some of the tables at the front of it, when I came across one entitled *Astronomical and Calendarial Data Sheet for 2007*. Not only did this table chart the dates of the full moon, but also the exact times of its zenith.

To my surprise and amazement, I noted that the highest point (or zenith) of the full moon on the previous morning had been at exactly 5.45 a.m. G.M.T. - just when I had encountered all the nature spirits in my garden. I simply couldn't believe the coincidence. I knew then why all the fairies and Elders had been in my back garden at that time.

They had come to celebrate the zenith of the full moon by having a huge party and celebration.

I was astonished on the one hand, and deeply touched and warmed by this thought on the other. I also realised why I hadn't seen anything at 3.00 a.m. when I first awoke. The spirits hadn't arrived from their own dimension at that stage in the night, since it was still too early - the moon hadn't quite reached its zenith.

I hope it is now obvious why I felt the need to include this magical experience in the book. The last coincidence made it simply impossible for me not to.

This encounter has been my most recent since all my visions began.

I don't know if I will ever again experience anything as vivid or compelling as I did during these encounters. It may be the case that nothing of significant note will occur for many years, as was the case with the *Little Boy*. Nothing happened for eleven years, and then unexpectedly, I experienced this intense six-month series of visions. All I can say, however, is that I have been deeply moved in a most positive way by all that has happened to me.

I must stress again that I was completely unprepared for much of what I saw and experienced through these encounters. I have always been an open-minded person, and a definite believer in the existence of a Spirit World, but even I was initially taken aback by my encounters with departed souls, elves and angels of Nature.

————————————

My final chapters make conclusions based on the content of the book. These have been divided into three main parts.

Chapter 8 discusses the encounters from Chapter 2 (*The Little Boy*) to Chapter 5 (*The Room*). I deal with such things as age discrepancy, and I discuss the existence of spiritual energy levels, and consider how these relate to humans when they enter the Spirit World upon their death.

Chapter 9 is concerned with the world of nature spirits (as described in the chapters *The Real Moon Fairy* and *The Party)*. It discusses the differences that exist between nature spirits and other spirit entities like the *Little Boy.*

Chapter 10 is entitled *'Final Thoughts'*, and in it I attempt to summarise my personal interpretation of these encounters. This chapter also discusses the most important messages I received from them.

The issues in my concluding chapters all arise directly from the encounters in the book, and I attempt to address as many relevant points as I can in relation to their themes.

Chapter 8

Conclusion - Part I

In this chapter, I discuss issues relating to Heaven and departed souls, raised in the chapters on the *Little Boy, The Wall, The Room* and *The Park.*

Some of what I say here may correlate with what other spiritual writers have said about these themes, while a lot of it may not. I must emphasise that I write directly from my own first-hand experiences, and do not claim to have the knowledge required to answer all the questions posed. At this time, I can only offer suggestions based on the impressions and knowledge I gained through my encounters.

I address some themes with more confidence and insight than others, and at times I am able to discount themes or issues that initially struck me as significant.

Why were the spirits different in age?

I strongly sensed that the spirits across *The Wall* were approximately thirty-three years old. I believe this age is very significant, and I gained the strong impression that many souls who depart earth arrive in the Spirit World and attain the comparable earthly age of thirty-three years, regardless of the age they died on earth.

Many of my encounters involved spirits who appeared at different ages, however, and I also wish to discuss some possible reasons for these variations.

I initially wondered why the spirits beyond *The Wall* were thirty-three years old as opposed to any other age. All I can perhaps assume is that thirty-three represents an age when most people are considered to be at their physical and mental prime on earth, and so this is perhaps the age many souls revert to in spirit.

This age is a defining one for many people here, as it often marks a time when they embark on things that determine the remainder of their lives (such as marriage, having children etc.). I also noted that this was the age Jesus died on earth, and so it perhaps has some symbolic or spiritual meaning that I am not fully aware of.

Although the spirits on Harry's particular energy level assumed this age, this may not necessarily be true for every energy level in the Spirit World. Why was it the case, for example, that certain spirits (like Grandpa Joe and the young man) appeared as both older and younger than thirty-three years old?

The young man in *The Park* died at the age of nineteen, yet I sensed he was about twenty-nine or thirty years old in my vision. I believe he hadn't reached the age of thirty-three because he had not entered one of the energy levels of Heaven proper.

I gained the impression that the young man was on some kind of ongoing journey - a point that troubled me during this particular encounter. He did not seem to have reached the more ideal level enjoyed by Harry and the other spirits beyond *The Wall,* and this made me wonder just exactly which level he had reached in the Spirit World.

I believe *The Park* represented a mid-way point between earth and the formal realms of Heaven. The young man appeared to find it difficult to move fully away from his life on earth, and he was therefore unable to completely embrace the Heavenly realms of existence.

I presume that his reticence was due to the sudden and premature nature of his death. He needed some time in the 'retaining area' of *The Park* to acclimatise and to spiritually mature and prepare himself for the formal realms of Heaven. Once he did this, he would then perhaps assume the more spiritually mature age of thirty-three.

This vision taught me that if a departed soul is still strongly linked to earth, then this hinders them from immediately entering an energy level proper. I gained the strong feeling that it is important for people grieving a loved one on earth to 'let go' of them, and pray for their safe, happy and peaceful journey to their final soul destination.

I recalled old sayings I had heard many times in the past (when people had died), such as "He/She is in a better place" or "Wish them well/onwards". These had once sounded so empty and clichéd to me, but they now suddenly seemed to make sense, especially in relation to my encounters at *The Park* and *The Wall*.

Grandpa Joe also appeared to me at a different age. He had died at the age of eighty-six, but appeared as a man of approximately sixty years old during my encounter. I believe he appeared to me at this age, however, so that I would *recognise* him. Had he appeared as a young, thirty-three year old man, I probably wouldn't have realised who he was, since I had only ever seen photographs of him as an old man in his eighties. He thus appeared between the ages of thirty-three (which I believe he may be in the actual Spirit World) and eighty-six years old (the age by which I knew him on earth).

It may be the case that Grandpa Joe *is* in fact approximately sixty years old in the actual Spirit World, and this may therefore suggest that he is more spiritually mature than the souls behind *The Wall*. So whilst age is constant within each particular energy level, differences may exist between these levels.

In a similar way, my vision of the *Little Boy* also threw up another age difference. This time the *Little Boy* was between six and eight years old. I believe this encounter was different to those in *The Park*, *The Room* and *The Wall*, however.

It seemed to me that the *Little Boy* was still part of a high spiritual energy level when he came to visit me, although I cannot claim to know anything about his exact place in the Spirit World. In my opinion, he was not incarnate on this earth for a very long time (whenever that may have been), and I strongly believe he is a spirit of peace and happiness, who has a particular spiritual role to play on earth. I don't believe the *Little Boy* needs to reach the age of thirty-three, however, and I somehow sense that he remains young because he has a particular job to with many people on earth.

It is also possible that he appeared as a child in order to enable those he visited to absorb the warmth, innocence, peace and spirituality exuded more by children than by adults.

What was the significance of the climate?

The climate I discerned as I was held outside *The Wall* was one of a warm, sunny environment, with temperatures pitched at around twenty-five degrees Celsius.

I believe there may be a very simple reason why I encountered this climate in the Spirit World. A warm, sunny environment is often considered to be pleasant and welcoming, and is perhaps more conducive to happiness, contentedness and productivity.

That is certainly the impression I received of life beyond *The Wall*. There was no indication that this climate ever changed, and all the spirits there seemed to be very at ease with their environment. Grandpa Joe's appearance via *The Room* also seemed to indicate his existence in a warm environment, something indicated by his attire and suntanned skin.

However, when I encountered the young man in *The Park*, he appeared to be experiencing a very oppressive and uncomfortable climate, but I believe there is a simple explanation for his overheating and tiredness on this occasion. During this encounter, I initially wondered why the young man seemed to find it so difficult to cope with the warm conditions, and I now believe this was due to the young man not having moved into an energy level proper. When the young man eventually moves away from *The Park* and discovers his true energy level in the Spirit World, I think he will be better able to cope with the climate, since he will then be a true spirit of light.

There may be another possible reason for the consistently warm and bright environment in the Spirit World, and this relates to the make-up of the spirit entities who reside there. Comprised of light energy, they may thrive, radiate and operate more efficiently in an atmosphere exuding light and warmth. These conditions are entirely consistent with their fabric.

At *The Wall*, I sensed a multitude of spirits who had (what I initially presumed to be) light-coloured skin and appearance. On reflection, however, I believe that this lightness was due to the energy or light emitted by each spirit entity, rather than their skin tone or colour.

Why are there different energy levels in Heaven?

Before my encounters, I always believed Heaven would be a place where one could roam freely from place to place, and meet at will, others who had previously passed away. I never embraced the concept of energy levels, nor did I ever consider the existence of work for spiritual advancement.

When I was held outside *The Wall*, I gained the strong impression that Harry and the other spirit souls had arrived at a particular energy level in the Spirit World. I strongly sensed that this was only one of many energy levels departed souls could enter.

I also felt that each spirit soul was directed to another place (I didn't know where) and given a particular spiritual job or task to do. I was told that this work would help them advance spiritually, and thus potentially help them rise through the various energy levels over time. Although I could not see the departed spirit souls in the other energy levels, I nevertheless strongly felt that their place or dimension was nearby.

So why do the multiple energy levels exist? I was able to find a possible reason for this from my encounter at *The Wall*. People who have lived their lives on earth pass into the Spirit World where they are given tasks or jobs to do. I don't know exactly what these jobs or tasks entail, except to say that they are spiritual in nature.

When I was permitted to look down at the earth during this encounter, I sensed the way a human lives their life on earth, dictates the energy level they enter the Spirit World upon their death. It is each person's relationship with other humans (and with the Spirit World above) that determines the spiritual energy level they eventually pass into. I can only presume that if we lead a spiritually guided, positive and prayerful life on earth, we are more likely to store up 'good' energy for our entry to the Spirit World (or Heaven) upon our death.

In Chapter 4 (*The Park*), the young man did not immediately enter an energy level proper. This was because he was sent to *The Park* to acclimatise and prepare for his entry into one of the many energy levels of Heaven.

Grandpa Joe, on the other hand, was obviously on a much higher energy level compared to the others. In fact, when I linked with him during my encounter, his energy nearly overwhelmed me.

It is important to note that I felt Grandpa Joe had somehow exited his energy level to link with me via *The Room*. I presume *The Room* he was in acted as some sort of intermediary vehicle, where links are endorsed or sanctioned by the Spirit World, and where communication and connections can be made with spirits on other energy levels.

I was not permitted to look directly into Harry's energy level across *The Wall*, while *The Room* also prevented me from seeing Grandpa Joe's true spiritual home. As an earthly soul with very low energy, I could not be allowed to see into either energy realm. I had not passed over to the other side, and so I did not belong on either of these spiritual levels. I was, however, permitted to see the young man in *The Park*, since he had not yet entered an energy level proper.

I am not sure what energy level the *Little Boy* belonged to. His visit brought me peace, calmness, warmth and happiness, so I presume his levels of spiritual energy must be very high.

My encounters taught me that energy levels do exist. They are inextricably linked to our human journey on earth, and also therefore to our soul essence in the Spirit World beyond. Earth is one of the lower energy levels (I was told this during my encounter at *The Wall*), but it is nevertheless bound up with, and helps determine, our spiritual life after death.

The unforgettable message I received (at *The Wall*) about the need for love and prayer was the most important lesson I took from this encounter. I sensed that it is extremely important for us to pray for spirits beyond the earth. It is also necessary for us to keep the links and lines of communication between Heaven and earth near and constant.

Why did time seem to slow down during some encounters and completely stop in others?

During my encounter with the *Little Boy*, I was encapsulated in a 'time bubble'. Time, from my perspective, stopped, and yet I sensed that earthly time outside the bubble went on as normal.

During my visit to *The Wall*, I again sensed that time stopped. Although I initially felt I had been at *The Wall* for quite a long time, I was in fact only away from the wake room for a few minutes.

Time also stopped when Grandpa Joe exited his energy level and linked with me via *The Room*. However, during my encounter with the young man in *The Park*, time *slowed down*, but did not stop completely (in relation to normal, earthly time).

Why then did I experience time slowing down in some encounters, and completely stopping in others?

During my encounter with the *Little Boy*, time stopped because I was incorporated into the energy of the *Little Boy*. If the *Little Boy* was my guardian angel, then he was an angel of light, and I was absorbed by that light.

During my visit to *The Wall*, I was brought to just outside the energy levels of Heaven. Here, departed souls were now spirits of light, and I was thus enveloped within their light energy.

During my encounter with Grandpa Joe, I was visited by a departed soul from a high energy level, and was again integrated into his light energy.

All of these encounters were with departed souls who had by now achieved very elevated levels of light energy. Time does not function where they exist, and I was lucky enough to sense this feeling of timelessness at first-hand. I believe I went through an *'out of normal-time experience'* on each of these occasions. I was able to encounter the timeless zone of the Spirit World as it exists outside of normal, earthly time.

In *The Park*, however, time did not completely cease to exist, but appeared to slow down. I believe the simple reason for this was due to the fact that the young man had not yet become a fully-fledged spirit of light energy.

My encounter with the *Real Moon Fairy* differed completely from all those discussed previously. During this encounter, time from my perspective did not become distorted or affected at all. This was because the *Moon Fairy* was an angel or spirit of Nature, and she could not therefore affect my experience of time. She had to enter *my* time realm, since I was unable as a human being to enter the realm of Nature and nature spirits which she occupied. She therefore had to enter *my* reality.

To summarise, when I was in very close contact with the spirits of light energy (such as the

Little Boy, Harry and Grandpa Joe), time stopped from my perspective. When I was in contact with the young man in *The Park*, time only slowed down partially. Why then the difference?

Anyone who has studied basic physics knows that if you boarded a rocket and accelerated enough, time would slow down, until it eventually stops at exactly the speed of light.

All encounters with spirits of light energy would alter the perception of time for anyone coming into contact with them: Being directly involved with a spirit of light energy would make time stop, whilst being indirectly involved would make time slow down, but not stop completely.

What was the significance of the red brick wall, blue sky

and green grass?

In Chapter 3 (*The Wall*) I describe how a large, red-brick wall separated me from the Spirit World.

This wall was approximately twenty feet in height. I could not see over it, but was able to look above and in front of it. Whilst I could not see beyond *The Wall*, I was nevertheless able to sense many things there, such as the climate and the existence of energy levels. I believe *The Wall* was made deliberately high so as to prevent me from directly seeing any of the departed spirit souls on the other side. If I had been able to see across it, then I believe I would not be writing this book, and that (quite simply) I would be dead! I was not a departed spirit soul and so could not be given access into any of the energy levels of the Spirit

World. I nevertheless feel extremely honoured and humbled to have had these experiences at all.

During my encounter at *The Wall*, when the souls on the other side discovered my presence, I was immediately whisked away for my own benefit. I felt as though I was some sort of honoured guest who was allowed to sense what was happening in the Spirit World for a short time only.

I believe that whoever (or whatever) brought me there insisted on the presence of this physical barrier to protect my psychological well-being. They knew that the image of the large, red-brick wall, with its accompanying green grass and blue sky, would make me feel comfortable and at ease. This sense of protection enabled me to fully absorb the information I was given from beyond *The Wall*.

I don't know whether the curved top had any spiritual significance, and it was perhaps simply there to soften the image of the wall itself.

Why were the departed souls across The Wall

similar in type?

I strongly sensed that Harry and the other departed souls across *The Wall* no longer looked human in form. I also felt that they were similar in design and spoke the same language.

Their uniform appearance makes total sense when one considers what likely happens to humans after death. When a human dies, they probably cease to exist in human form, and henceforth assume a new appearance or structure in their new spiritual realm. Each departed human soul must adopt a new energy profile or contour, which is determined by the energy level they now reside on in Heaven.

Since departed souls are comprised of light energy, they must be 'One' in every way. That is why, I believe, they are similar in design and speak the same language; they are now light beings living in a light energy realm. However, since there are multiple energy levels, then there must also be several types of light being. These entities probably possess varying quantities of light energy, depending upon which level in the Spirit World they belong to.

Grandpa Joe is a light being with much more energy than the young man in *The Park*. His energy is very high and he can (I sense) move into an energy level lower than his own. Whether this is always done directly, or via an area like *The Room*, I am not completely sure. I do feel, however, that departed souls with lower light energy cannot access or move directly into a higher energy realm. It is possible, however, that they eventually move into the higher levels through constant prayer and spiritual work.

Whilst I did not look into the Spirit World itself, I was nevertheless able to see Grandpa Joe and the young man thanks to the connecting agencies of *The Room* and *The Park*. I do not believe, however, that their appearance on each of these occasions was necessarily how they would appear in the actual energy realms of the Spirit World.

I instinctively believe spirit souls re-assume a form that resembles their once earthly appearance during their spiritual visitations. This is to ensure they are recognised by those they appear to on an earthly level.

However, I believe they possibly revert to their spiritual appearance (whatever that is) after their visitation. It could be that their spiritual appearance is not very far removed from their humanly appearance, but I am not able to make any firm assertions on this point.

What was the significance of the elves that accompanied Grandpa Joe in The Room?

I was completely unprepared for the band of enchanting, mischievous elves that accompanied Grandpa Joe in *The Room*. The first thing I remarked about them was the manner in which they seemed to be intrinsically connected to the essence or spirit of the man himself. Their characteristics very closely mirrored or mimicked Grandpa Joe's mischievous, fun-loving nature.

I wondered whether the elves were simply there for Grandpa Joe's amusement, since they did truly seem to be at his beck-and-call. I then began to think of another possible theory. It could perhaps be the case that when Grandpa Joe's spirit became physically manifest via the medium of *The Room*, it did so in two main parts. The first was Grandpa Joe's physical form as it had appeared on earth, whilst the second took the form of the elves, which emerged physically and tangibly as part of his spirit, essence or personality.

In other words, it is not necessarily the case that elves exist physically in the Spirit World beyond *The Room*. When Grandpa Joe returns there, his spirit perhaps merges with the energy or spirit of his elves, and he once again becomes a completely intact, spiritual entity of light. Thus, Grandpa Joe's spirit perhaps incorporates (or is infused with) that of the elves in the actual Spirit World. It could be the case that the elves are an integral part of Grandpa Joe's essence, and when he appeared in *The Room*, part of his energy 'broke off' to form the elves. This 'break-off' could be Grandpa Joe's essence or personality manifesting in physical form, separate to his more recognisable human body. I have heard through stories and anecdotes about Grandpa Joe that he was most definitely a 'larger-than-life' character.

I wondered whether these elves had been part of Grandpa Joe's life when he had lived on earth. I also questioned the possibility that we are all, in some way or other, accompanied by a variety of spirit entities, such as elves and fairies (or indeed other spirit forces whose power or influence we may not even know about). These may reflect or determine our own appearance, personality, essence and spirit as it exists on earth, and then also in the Spirit World upon our death.

I considered the possibility that we adopt these entities or spirits as we go through life on earth. It could of course be the case that Grandpa Joe's particular elves represented his creative energy - just in the same way the elves assisted the shoemaker in the well-known fairy tale.

Most of the visions occurred on a Monday. Does this day have any special significance?

Most of my encounters took place on a Monday, and I wondered whether this day held any particular significance.

When I embarked upon some research on this issue, I discovered many facts about Monday. I initially found out that the word comes from the Anglo-Saxon term 'Mōnandæg', meaning '*day of the moon*'. Monday can be regarded as either the first or second day of the week, depending upon what part of the world you live in, or what religion you belong to. Monday (or *Moon day*) is obviously strongly linked to the moon, and I used this as a starting point to see if any connection existed between the dates when the visions occurred, and the phases of the moon at those particular times. When I checked, I found the moon phases to be different on each date, so no correlation appeared to exist. I also checked to see if Monday had any specific religious significance, but again I found none.

After going down several other different avenues with no luck, I realised that the reason why many of my encounters took place on a Monday was probably much simpler than I had initially contemplated.

Monday is the day I go back to work after my weekend break. I know I am much more relaxed at weekends, and have more time to ponder life in general. I realised that I had initially linked with the Spirit World during these calmer moments. I recalled the weekend before the encounter with Grandpa Joe, when I had sensed the spirits so overwhelmingly, I had to ask them to leave.

It seemed that when I was relaxed during weekends my association with the Spirit World became very strong, and this connection culminated by each Monday.

Thus, there is a more practical reason (rather than a symbolic, historical or religious one) why most of my encounters occurred on a Monday.

Why did the visions appear on my right- hand side?

The young man, Grandpa Joe, Harry and the other spirits emerged and appeared on my right-hand side. Again, I pondered the significance of this fact, and once more undertook a little research.

There are many references in the Bible to people or things at God's Right Hand, but I came up with no solid reason as to why the encounters always appeared on my right-hand side.

Why was there an intense smell associated
with some of the encounters?

A very strong and distinctive smell accompanied my encounters with Grandpa Joe in *The Room* and the young man in *The Park*. This smell penetrated my head on each occasion, and acted as a forewarning to the encounters themselves.

I believe my senses were brought into very sharp focus before and during these encounters, and this increased sensitivity was probably due to the very strong spiritual connection I forged with the young man and Grandpa Joe. On both of these occasions, I detected an odour which resembled old, musty books or an old, musty room whose door had not been opened for a very long time.

During my encounter with Grandpa Joe, my senses peaked at an all-time high. In fact, I could sense the peculiar, musty smell several days before the actual encounter. There were several other occasions when I sensed this intense smell (and was able to feel the presence of other spirit souls nearby), but did not necessarily have an actual, visual encounter.

This smell undoubtedly formed part of my connection with the Spirit World, and the more intensely I experienced it, the stronger I connected with the spirit souls.

What I did note, however, was that I did not hear any sounds during most of my encounters. Indeed, the only occasion when I was clairaudient was at *The Party*.

Chapter 9

Conclusion - Part II

A number of questions arose from my encounters with the *Real Moon Fairy* and the nature spirits at *The Party*.

Who exactly was the Real Moon Fairy?

The *Moon Fairy* was a tiny, androgynous, deva spirit of Nature. She appeared along with her Orb as a direct result of my faith in her and others of her kind. She was not a human spirit, nor had she *ever* been part of the human race. This was the only time I encountered an entity with wings, and I therefore firmly believe *The Real Moon Fairy* was part of Nature itself.

She was in total charge of the Orb, which contained the multitude of tiny nature spirit entities. On the night we met, the *Moon Fairy* brought the Orb entities along with her in order to let them see what a human being was like. She only did this, I believe, because she understood my *true faith* in her existence (and in the tiny entities in the Orb). She knew that my faith would honour her presence.

What did the Moon Fairy look like?

As soon as the *Moon Fairy* appeared to me, I immediately recognised her from images I had seen somewhere before. Her face bore a striking resemblance to the faces carved on the statues on Easter Island in the Pacific Ocean. This uncanny likeness compelled me to look into possible connections between the *Moon Fairy* and Easter Island.

Easter Island (also known as Rapa Nui) contains approximately 800 large stone statues. These statues (known as 'Moai' statues) stand on stone platforms called 'ahu'. The Moai and ahu were used on the island as early as AD 500, and most were carved between the dates AD 100 and AD 1650.

In ancient Polynesian religions, carved stone and wooden objects were thought to be charged with a magical spirit called 'mana'. These statues were apparently carved as symbols of religious and political authority, and were regarded as the repositories of sacred spirits.

Whilst the statues of Rapa Nui have been toppled and rebuilt over the centuries, their mana is still strongly present.

Although I have no proof of any connection between the *Moon Fairy* who appeared to me and the faces on the sacred statues on Rapa Nui, I cannot help but think that the ancients and spiritualists who lived there generations ago perhaps also had encounters with devas and nature spirits in the same way I did.

What about the Moon Fairy's companions in the Orb?

The Orb was a collective of spirit energies controlled by the *Moon Fairy*. Both entities travelled via wisps of light; these clearly linked them to a different energy level. They appeared to emerge from inside the realms of Nature, and so their arrival did not distort my experience of human, earthly time.

The Orb's tiny spirit entities were like juvenile devas from the world of Nature. I believe these tiny, child-like entities also appeared alongside the other nature spirits at *The Party*. The Orb was the same colour as the *Moon Fairy*, so I assume they were related, although I don't know exactly how.

What else is known about Orbs? The word comes from the Latin 'Orbis', meaning 'round object'. Photographs of Orbs reveal they are often accompanied by trails or wisps of light, and it is thought they most commonly appear during early morning and evening (mine appeared in the early morning). Numerous photographs indicate the presence of Orbs near people who have lost loved ones, and this again links them to the Spirit World.

Although it is not the purpose of this book to write at length about Orbs, most writers on this subject believe there are many different types. Orbs appear to have many spiritual functions - including work with guardian angels, departed souls, spirit guides and nature spirits.

Chapter 10

Final Thoughts

I began to write this book as a record of my spiritual encounters. My most important objective was to share these experiences in the hope that their messages would help and inspire others.

The book spans eleven years. It begins with my encounter with a *Little Boy*, whom I subsequently realised was my guardian angel. The *Little Boy* appeared as a prelude to my future encounters. Although I didn't recognise the true significance of this encounter at the time, I have since reflected at length about the importance of angels, spirit guides and guardian angels.

I now believe the *Little Boy* came in order to prepare me in advance for the other spiritual encounters I would have.

I have recognised, through my encounters, the close proximity we humans have with angels. They are there to be called upon in times of need, and they want us to speak to them and ask for their help and guidance. Guardian angels look after all our well-being. They may not physically appear to everyone, but this doesn't mean they are not present. Angels frequently assist us in very subtle ways without us even realising it, so all we need to do is ask for their help, and wait for it to arrive.

One of the most important things I share in the book is my encounter with the Spirit World at *The Wall*; I was able to make a number of observations on this occasion. I gauged that human souls enter one of many *energy levels* in Heaven upon their death, where they become spirit entities comprised (in varying degrees) of love and light. The energy level they enter is decided and based upon the goodness and quality of life they lived on earth.

It is my strong belief that spirit souls remain connected to life on earth. Their 'death' on this level of existence simply represents their passing on to another more elevated spiritual realm. They have a different role or job to do elsewhere, but that does not mean they have gone; indeed, this could not be further from the truth.

This point is of great significance to those of us who experience the loss of a loved one on earth as all of us have, or will do, at some point in our lives.

Our very strong connection to the Spirit World, through the angelic realms and the world of nature spirits, is the most profound and important message I received during all my encounters. I strongly sensed that everybody on earth is a spirit in human form. We are created in Heaven and we will all return there some day. Since we are human by nature, we often become distracted by material, physical and non-spiritual beliefs and practices during our stay on this planet.

We frequently lose touch with the things that should be most important in our lives, namely our spiritual well-being and our deep connection to Heaven and the Spirit World. These things surround us every moment of our lives, if we could only recognise them more often.

The vision I had of a grey and sick Planet Earth as I stood outside *The Wall*, represented, I believe, the manner in which many of us have lost touch with our inner spirit and our spiritual journey on earth. I received a very strong message about the importance of prayer during this encounter, and about the need for faith in Heaven and the angelic realms. I was unequivocally told there is a need for greater spiritual communication on *all* levels of existence.

Our lives on earth are intrinsically linked with the energy levels of Heaven above. We are all spiritual entities (in human form), and we each have a spiritual role to play on earth. My encounters with the spirits of Nature (like the *Real*

Moon Fairy and the various entities at *The Party*) also drew my attention to the importance of our connection with Nature and the environment, and of our need to cherish and look after this planet and everything on it.

All our actions and thoughts impact upon others on earth, and upon the universe and Spirit World beyond this planet. We are like energy forms that emit, through our every thought and deed, various types of energy. This resonates in either a positive or negative manner on all other energy forms, depending upon the intention behind the thought or deed.

Everything we do, say, think or contemplate has a knock-on effect, such is our deep spiritual connectedness with each other and everything. Our adherence to material practices and beliefs on earth must not be allowed to overtake or conceal our spiritual lives both here and beyond.

We each have a particular role to play on earth, and it is likely that this was pre-determined in some way before we came here. Spiritual work can sometimes involve negative thoughts and deeds, but these must also be viewed as having potentially important spiritual outcomes. It is often the case that negative, hurtful and evil actions inspire very positive behaviour in others, such as courage, love and forgiveness. It is important for us to rise above our initial human reactions of revenge or hate, therefore, when we experience the negative actions of people.

This is of course very, very difficult to do at times, but our angels and the other spiritual entities are there to help and guide us if we ask for their assistance. They can encourage us to forgive the spirit energy committing the negative deed, and help us to restore positive energy to the planet. In this way, we can avoid cluttering the earth with more negative energy in the form of grudges and anger. Frequent prayer and meditation can help us to achieve these goals. As I discovered at *The Wall*, the more positive energy we attain on earth, the higher the energy level we enter Heaven upon our death.

The familiar analogy of the small ripple in a large lake, spreading further and further outwards, is apt in describing how both our positive and negative deeds and thoughts impact well beyond our immediate environment.

Just as our actions and thoughts have a profound significance and effect on the world around us, so too does our death or departure from earth. It is as much a part of our lives as our birth, or all the other bits in between.

Humans have great difficulty coming to terms with death. The sense of loss and sadness we feel when a loved one dies can sometimes overwhelm us to the point of despair. We become angry, confused, afraid, hurt and inconsolable because we cannot understand why it had to happen - especially if the death was very sudden or tragic (as with cases of suicide, young deaths, still-birth or miscarriage). Most of all, we wonder if we will ever meet our loved ones again.

If I can say anything relating to this last point from my encounters, then the answer is undoubtedly '*Yes*', we will all meet up again when the time comes. Our loved ones are never far away. They have moved to another realm of existence where they have other spiritual work to do for now. They exist in that lovely environment of light and contentedness where time does not exist. Although we may miss them, and while waiting to see them again feels like forever on our earthly time level, they live only for the moment in their higher realm.

They are entirely happy, so we don't need to worry about them. We are only mourning for our own sense of loss from an earthly perspective when we feel sad, lonely and hurt at their passing.

This is all very easy to say of course. It takes a lot of courage and a huge leap of faith to see beyond our own sense of physical loss to the wider spiritual significance of someone's death on earth. It is, however, the only real way to understand and come to terms with every single death on this planet.

Human beings should not worry about death because our loved ones who have passed away have returned to where they, and the rest of us, came from. They chose (like us) to come to earth for a specific reason, and for a particular time, to enhance their own spirituality and to affect other human souls around them.

Being 'dead' is just the view from a human perspective. In reality, their souls have returned to where they came from, and they have now acquired eternal peace and happiness. Humans should be very happy and rejoice when a friend or loved one passes away because their specific task here is done. So when a person dies young, we should be grateful for what they have given to us during their short stay on earth. They will have affected all our lives in some way, either directly or indirectly. Their purpose will have been to change or shape the quality of life for their friends and family, so that they in turn may move on to repeat the process.

Sometimes the more tragic, inexplicable or premature a death is, the more profound meaning it has for those left behind on earth. It may result in medical research and thus save or enhance the lives of others in the future. It may inspire someone to positively change direction in life, or quite simply, the soul may have been called to do important spiritual work in the Heavenly realms of existence.

We may not be able to know or see these things at the time, but it is all for a very good reason. In the meantime, we can continue to stay connected to them through prayer and with the help of angels.

Death often leaves behind extremely strong bonds which take a very long time to heal. Because of this, the spirit soul who has passed away may not immediately enter an energy level proper, and may remain in another realm (such as *The Park*) for some time to acclimatise after leaving the energy level of earth behind.

Through time and lots of prayer, the spirit soul may eventually pass into one of the numerous energy levels of Heaven. This is obviously good for the spirit soul, and for their friends and family who have been left behind on earth. It is thus very important for us to release them from their earthly bonds.

We are in essence away from our real home when we decide to come and live a life on earth, but we will all return there some day to a glorious homecoming and reunion. I sensed Harry and the others experiencing a deep sense of happiness, welcome and fulfilment upon their arrival in Heaven beyond *The Wall*.

It put me in mind of a particular piece of scripture I happened to come across. It is taken from *Psalm 21, verse 2*:

"You welcomed him with a multitude of blessings,

And set a crown of pure gold on his head.

He asked for life, and you gave it,

A long and lasting life"

We will all be welcomed back some day in such a manner.

The purpose of writing this book was to share my encounters with Heaven and the Spirit World with others. At one point, I found it quite difficult to keep going, so I asked for some guidance from above as to whether or not I should complete the book.

Having been inspired (through my encounters) to read about angels, I came across the idea that they can communicate with us by leaving signs such as white feathers. So I asked for a sign in the form of a white feather to indicate whether or not I should continue with the book.

I deliberately looked around, but couldn't find one anywhere. After a day or so, I happened to walk upstairs into my bedroom, and by chance I looked out of the window.

In front of me, was a beautiful, clear sky - except for one large cloud straight ahead. It was in the shape of a beautiful white feather, and it was unmistakeable. I instinctively knew then that I must continue with the book, in the hope of helping at least one other person on earth through doing so.

This book has posed a lot of questions for me, most of them very personal and spiritual in nature. I wondered why all of this happened to me, and questioned why I was permitted to see, not only where human souls go to after death, but also how the spirits of Nature exist. I also still wonder about who it was brought me to *The Wall.*

I still don't fully know the answers to many of these questions, but I have shared all of my encounters in as truthful and accurate a manner as possible.

We co-exist with the Spirit World on many levels, including the realm of angels, departed souls and nature spirits. I don't know if I will have further spiritual encounters, but if I was permitted to discover one more thing, then it would be to know that the young man has found his rightful destination in the Spirit World after spending time in *The Park*.

My entire existence and outlook on life has changed profoundly, and for the better, since having these encounters. It was deeply uplifting to experience at first hand how close we *all* are to these spirit entities.

The Origins of Elves & Fairies
by joseph martin

The Origins of Elves & Fairies has been a widely debated topic for many generations. This book provides a fascinating insight into the realm of nature spirits, and examines the profound connection human beings can have with these entities. By exploring how, where and when we encounter the spirits of Nature, the book offers an entirely unique approach to understanding the world of elves and fairies. Even more importantly, it considers what our spiritual connection with the spirits of Nature signifies for our human soul.

- Learn where, when and how we are most likely to connect with elves, fairies and other nature spirits.

- Read the author's first-person accounts of actual elf and fairy encounters, and learn what is meant by the *energy profile* theory.

- Find out why elves and fairies look and behave the way they do.

- Discover how and why elves, fairies and other nature spirits attach themselves to our human spirit.

- Be aware of the importance of connecting with Nature in daily life.

- Read about how and why nature spirits can join us in the Spirit World after our death on earth.

- Learn about the significance of dance, movement, rhythm and music in nature spirit encounters.

Discover an entirely fresh approach to understanding these wonderful entities of Nature and in doing so, discover yourself ...

Angels Devas & Orbs
by joseph martín

Angels, Devas & Orbs is the third in a trilogy of books relating to the theme of nature spirits. It touches upon many of the author's personal spiritual encounters, including those with the Spirit World, and many from the world of Nature itself. The book explores in detail how nature spirit entities such as elves, fairies and orbs interact with human beings – both on an earthly level and in the Spirit World (or Heaven) itself. It offers a detailed discussion of many of the themes relating to this increasingly popular topic in current spiritual writing. joseph martín's observations and theories are unique; they arise from his personal encounters with the spirits of Nature, and from his experiences with many other spiritual realms of existence.

The book includes-

- A detailed description of an angel of Nature (or deva).

- A detailed description of an orb encounter.

- A considered explanation about why devas and angels have wings - including their possible spiritual function.

- A discussion about the spiritual significance and function of orbs.

- The author's first-hand observations regarding the hierarchies that exist within the realm of nature spirits.

- A detailed discussion about the lemniscate's role in facilitating spiritual encounters between humans, devas, orbs and other nature spirits.

- How the earth's spirituality can increase in line with the much-debated 2012 phenomenon.